# THE ART OF ABSTRACTION

A Practical Guide to Mastering Generalization

Jeremy Nixon

# The Art of Abstraction: A Practical Guide to Mastering Generalization

Jeremy Nixon

# Table of Contents

# Chapter 1

# Understanding Abstraction: The Key to Managing Complexity

Abstraction is a powerful tool that enables us to harness the complexity of the world, transforming it into digestible chunks that can be processed, understood, and acted upon. By creating mental models, we can transcend the overwhelming volume of information and cognitive demand that defines modern life, empowering ourselves to make thoughtful, informed decisions that account for the interdependencies and intricacies of our surroundings.

To gain a more profound understanding of abstraction in action, consider the task of navigating a bustling city. The environment is teeming with sensory stimuli, innumerable roads and pathways, and countless individuals, each with unique goals and perspectives. How can we hope to approach such an overwhelmingly complex landscape? Certainly not by trying to account for every single detail. Instead, we rely on abstraction, breaking down the city into its constituent parts - neighborhoods, blocks, and streets.

By mapping out these interconnected components, we enable ourselves to focus on specific, tractable aspects of the landscape while preserving the ability to understand the city as a whole. Abstraction, in this sense, allows us to balance the competing needs of simplicity and complexity, guiding our interactions with the world while keeping our cognitive faculties intact.

A striking example of abstraction applied to more technical domains is the field of computer science, in which programmers must grapple with vast, intricate systems characterized by numerous interdependent variables and processes. By employing abstraction, computer scientists can develop algorithms and data structures that simplify these interactions, breaking them down into computationally tractable tasks that can be executed efficiently and effectively.

Consider, for instance, how abstraction allows us to streamline the development of software. By partitioning our codebase into distinct functions and modules, we can isolate specific concerns, simplifying the overall structure of the system and mitigating the risk of unintentional interference between components. This enables developers to reason about smaller, more focused pieces, which are far easier for the human mind to comprehend than the entirety of the codebase. Moreover, abstraction accords us the ability to reuse components in multiple solutions, greatly enhancing the efficiency of our development efforts.

Despite its many advantages, abstraction is not without its challenges. As we simplify and generalize our models, it is critical that we preserve the essential details that are necessary for effective decision-making. In the realm of software development, this may involve representing crucial structures within a system, such as intricate call graphs or dependency relations that lie at the core of the application. Abstraction, in this sense, is an exercise in balance: we must strike the right equilibrium between accessibility and accuracy, ensuring that the vital elements of our models remain intact while trimming away the extraneous details that add complexity and hinder understanding.

Navigating this balance is not always easy, and it requires an ongoing process of reflection, experimentation, and adaptation, as well as a keen understanding of the underlying assumptions that drive our abstraction efforts. By continually reassessing and refining our mental models, we afford ourselves the opportunity to develop deep, nuanced understandings of the complex systems that define our world, empowering us to make informed, responsible decisions that account for the emergent properties and intricate interrelationships that drive change and innovation.

Understanding abstraction, then, is the key to managing complexity in our increasingly connected, information-rich world. By harnessing the power of abstraction, we can develop the cognitive infrastructure necessary to comprehend the vast and intricate landscapes that surround us- be they bustling cities or elaborate software systems - and make sense of the world in a way that is simultaneously simplifying and deeply insightful.

Armed with this knowledge, we can look forward to exploring the varieties of abstraction that pervade our reality and mastering the techniques necessary to manage complexity and excel in a world defined by extraordinary intricacy and seemingly infinite detail. It is through abstraction that we will come to profoundly understand the phenomena that define our existence, invigorated by the rich tapestry of interwoven structures, patterns, and relations that compose the fabric of our world.

## Introduction to Abstraction: Managing Complexity in a Complex World

In a world defined by its infinite complexities, we find ourselves navigating webs of intricacies, where even a single thread can lead us down a path of subtle contradictions and hidden relationships. As humans, our capacity for making sense of these complexities is limited; however, our intellect provides us with the means to manage and comprehend such a world. One of the critical aspects of this human intellect is the ability to abstract - to distill essential details from a sea of complexity, enabling us to make sense of the world around us.

Abstraction, at its core, is the process of filtering out peripheral information and highlighting the elements that truly matter in a given context. For instance, when we encounter a new program or algorithm, we don't attempt to understand every line of code; instead, we isolate core functionality, seeking to gather an overview of how the program works and its purpose. By focusing on the essential aspects, we simplify the complexity, allowing us to process and understand it effectively.

A recurring example of abstraction in the realm of computer science can be observed in object - oriented programming (OOP), a paradigm that encourages programmers to create modular designs, each serving a specific purpose. Programmers group objects with similar properties and methods as classes, defining the relationships between them and building hierarchies. In this way, OOP allows developers to manage complex codebases by breaking down the problem into simpler, more manageable components.

But abstraction extends far beyond the realm of computer science. It plays a fundamental role in all areas of human endeavor, from chemistry, where the periodic table serves as an abstraction of chemical elements, to economics, where idealized models such as supply and demand curves guide our understanding of economic systems. Moreover, abstraction has a long history in the world of mathematics - think back to Euclid, who laid the foundation for modern geometry by abstracting from the tangible world to the realm of ideas, or to the later developments of algebra, where letters and symbols represent abstracted quantities and relationships.

The power of abstraction becomes most apparent when confronting problems that require us to make connections between seemingly unrelated concepts, or when faced with situations where no straightforward solution presents itself. Deep Learning, a subset of machine learning, provides a fascinating example of the use of abstraction to deal with large-scale, complex problems in Artificial Intelligence (AI). By employing neural networks, developers create multilayered systems capable of identifying patterns and trends in vast quantities of data, effectively abstracting higher-level insights and knowledge. Deep Learning has led to groundbreaking advances in fields as diverse as natural language processing, computer vision, and self-driving vehicles.

However, abstraction is not without its challenges. In our quest for simplicity, we sometimes run the risk of oversimplifying, discarding information that may prove essential to a proper understanding of a problem. Alternatively, we may remain too attached to details, failing to see the broader patterns that could guide us toward a more effective approach. Striking the right balance between simplification and the retention of essential information is an art that demands thoughtfulness, careful assessment, and the ability to make well-founded judgments.

As we move through this intricate world, our ability to embrace abstraction becomes vital to our effectiveness and success. Whether through navigating new technologies, dissecting complex algorithms, or finding innovative solutions to age-old problems, abstraction serves as a powerful tool in our cognitive arsenal.

## The Importance of Identifying Shared Structures and Discarding Superfluous Details

In a world saturated with information and complexities, problem - solvers of today face a unique challenge: to decipher meaning through the noise. Traditionally, this requires the skilled manipulation of abstraction and simplification, identifying shared structures and discarding superfluous details. How can we best execute this delicate dance of abstraction?

Perhaps a useful starting point would be to visualize the task at hand as solving a labyrinthine jigsaw puzzle. Spread before us is a vast array of seemingly unrelated, irregularly shaped pieces. As we approach the task, we must rely on our cognitive abilities to discern patterns among these fragments. Through comparison and analysis, we discover their shared structures: the correspondent shapes, colors, and textures that allow each piece to interlock with others. Simultaneously, we learn to discard the misleading and irrelevant elements - the odd images, incomplete lines, or peculiar shapes - with the ultimate aim of constructing a coherent picture from the disjointed components.

The importance of identifying shared structures cannot be underestimated. Consider the field of software architecture, in which complex applications are built from myriad code fragments. By applying abstraction principles to these fragments, software architects can identify recurring programming patterns, thus allowing for the development of reusable components that can be applied throughout the application. By reusing these components and embracing modular design, efficiency and consistency are maximized, while redundancy is minimized.

For example, imagine a programmer tasked with creating an e-commerce website. This program's shared structures might include data handling routines, user authentication mechanisms, and a uniform graphical user interface. By identifying these overlapping elements, the programmer can develop a toolbox of modules, each designed to perform a specific task, which can be combined to create the complete application. This process of identification and the creation of shared structures pave the way for more efficient programming and better - structured systems.

However, engaging with abstraction in the pursuit of shared structures is only half the battle. Equally important is our ability to discard superfluous details, the extraneous elements that would otherwise obscure our understanding of the core problem. Discarding these details allows us to maintain focus on the essential aspects of a problem or situation, preventing us from being overwhelmed, and enabling a faster resolution.

In the realm of data science, for example, researchers often grapple with vast datasets to uncover trends and correlations. However, not all details in the datasets are relevant, and an excess of superfluous information can create a 'signal-to-noise' ratio imbalance. Discarding non-essential details while retaining those that are useful and relevant is crucial for preserving the meaningfulness of the insights gleaned from the data. This process of purposeful omission is not only applicable to data science but also to fields as diverse as statistical modeling, strategic planning, and product development.

Continuing with the example of the e-commerce website, the programmer is likely to encounter many irrelevant details, such as infrequently used features, excessive customization options, or convoluted user flows. Recognizing these as distractions, the programmer must learn to discard them, ensuring that the core functionality remains smooth, efficient, and streamlined.

In both identifying shared structures and discarding the superfluous, the key to achieving successful abstraction lies in the art of discrimination, distinguishing those details essential to accurately represent a problem or a process from those that may mislead or overcomplicate. As we immerse ourselves in tackling the complex issues of the modern world, our ability to nimbly navigate the intricacies of abstraction may well hold the key to future problem-solving successes.

As we progress to explore the various forms of abstraction and learn how they can be harnessed across disparate fields, it is essential to remember that the power of abstraction is tightly bound to its responsible application. As we abstract further into understanding the grand puzzle of the world, the delicate balance between simplification and retaining essential details will prove pivotal in unlocking our ability to truly manage complexities in a complex world.

## Varieties of Abstraction: Exploring the Different Forms and Their Subtle Differences

In the realm of abstraction, we often find ourselves pondering the nature of complex and multifaceted systems. Whether it be the framework of an AI prototype, the intricate web of global economies, or the rulebook that governs the game of cricket, we inevitably employ abstraction to make sense of it all. Yet, as we stand before the canvas of varying abstraction types, a veritable smorgasbord of forms and subtle differences emerges.

Take, for instance, the abstract realm of mathematics. We deal with numbers, variables, and equations that are far-removed from the physical world, yet they become foundational for our comprehension of complex phenomena. This mathematical abstraction plays an essential role in quantitative finance, as sophisticated models allow us to predict stock prices, identify opportunities for investment, and manage risks with incredible precision.

Consider, on the other hand, a literary critic engaging with the dense prose of James Joyce's Ulysses. Here, the abstraction arises from breaking down complex narrative structures, analyzing overarching themes, and parsing symbolic language to uncover the author's intended meaning. While the tools may be vastly different, the essence of abstraction in literary analysis shares the same goal as mathematical abstraction: to distill complex information and capture the essence of the subject matter.

Now, let us turn our attention to the world of software engineering. Here lies a treasure trove of abstraction types, from functional abstraction, which captures the essence of computation, to modular abstraction, which allows us to manage complexity by decomposing systems into smaller, more manageable components. These seemingly disparate forms of abstraction come together in harmony, much like an expertly conducted symphony, to enable the creation of robust and efficient software systems.

Abstraction in scientific modeling presents yet another exciting frontier. Imagine a meteorologist seeking to predict the behavior of a hurricane - a phenomenon fraught with chaotic interactions of myriad variables. To do so, they must embrace physical abstraction, stripping away non-essential details of the real world so that the storm's core dynamics can be captured in a computer simulation. This allows for critical insights and forecasts that would be otherwise unattainable.

As we delve deeper into these varieties of abstraction, the richness of their nuances becomes apparent. Recursive abstraction allows us to discover patterns and relationships within complex data, while temporal abstraction gives us the power to distill the essence of time - varying processes. In a dance of interwoven complexity, these forms of abstraction merge and transform, creating a dynamic kaleidoscope of cognitive tools that empower us to make sense of our world.

As our journey reaches its conclusion, let us reflect on the key lessons we have learned. Embracing the various facets of abstraction enables us to conquer the intellectual Everest, scaling the dizzying heights of complexity with relative ease. As we sharpen our minds to perceive the subtle differences and strengths of each abstraction form, we unlock new pathways for problem - solving and innovation.

Yet, we must not leave uncharted the potential pitfalls of abstraction. Taken too far, the allure of simplicity can blind us to essential nuances, leaving us vulnerable to oversimplification and the risk of misunderstanding. Our voyage of discovery now behind us, we are called to wield the power of abstraction with skill and mindfulness, carefully navigating the balance between essence and detail to unleash our problem - solving prowess.

## Abstraction in Action: Examples from Computer Science, Deep Learning, and Conceptual Reasoning

Abstraction is a powerful technique that has transformed the way we approach problems in various fields, including computer science, deep learning, and conceptual reasoning. By examining examples from these disciplines, we can appreciate how abstraction has profoundly impacted our lives and contributed to countless advances in technology and knowledge.

One of the most well - known instances of abstraction in computer science is the creation of programming languages. Early computers required humans to interact with them using machine code - a daunting tasks for even the most dedicated programmer. As programming languages evolved, they incorporated higher levels of abstraction that simplified the process and allowed programmers to write more complex and powerful applications without concerning themselves with the minutiae of machine - code instructions.

Take, for example, the development of high-level programming languages like Java, Python, and JavaScript. These languages allow developers to focus on solving the problems at hand, instead of worrying about the low-level details of computer memory management or implementing complex algorithms from scratch. The principles of functional and object-oriented programming further abstract the code into reusable modules, which can be combined and reused to create complex software systems. This simplification and modularization have facilitated the creation of some of the world's most popular and innovative software applications and systems, from operating systems to web applications and beyond.

Deep learning, a subfield of artificial intelligence, also heavily relies on abstraction for its remarkable achievements. Neural networks, the central component of deep learning systems, are abstract models inspired by the way biological brains process information. These networks consist of interconnected layers of neurons, with information flowing from one layer to the next to accomplish tasks such as object recognition, language translation, and playing strategy games.

At the core of the deep learning revolution lies the concept of representation learning: constructing features or representations from raw input data, often through abstraction. This process allows deep learning models to tackle complex problems in a hierarchical and structured manner, leveraging the powerful idea of abstraction in the data itself. For example, when training a neural network to recognize images of animals, the initial layers might abstract the image into primitive shapes, such as lines and edges. These elements are then combined and further abstracted in subsequent layers to represent more complex structures, such as eyes, noses, and fur patterns, eventually enabling the model to distinguish a cat from a dog.

Regardless of the specific application, deep learning relies on abstraction to achieve its remarkable success, providing a glimpse into the potential for abstraction to transform problem-solving in other domains as well.

In the realm of conceptual reasoning, abstraction plays a pivotal role in shaping our understanding and navigation of the world. When facing a seemingly insurmountable problem, we often break it down into smaller, more manageable components - a process known as decomposition. Once we've achieved a solution at this more abstract level, we can then synthesize and apply the insights back to the original problem. This process of deconstruction, abstraction, and reintegration facilitates profound advancements in our ability to reason and solve complex problems.

Take, for instance, the field of mathematics, where abstraction enables us to recognize and manipulate patterns between seemingly disparate ideas or objects. This skill, often referred to as mathematical intuition, allows mathematicians to discover profound truths and connections by examining problems from unique and abstract perspectives. Similarly, in the world of philosophy, thinkers apply abstraction to fundamental questions of existence, ethics, and knowledge, engaging in deep discussions and debates that lead to new and impactful ideas about the nature of our reality.

These examples, drawn from computer science, deep learning, and conceptual reasoning, illustrate the immense power and potential of abstraction as a problem-solving tool. As we continue to develop and hone our skills in abstract thinking, we unlock new possibilities for the creative and innovative application of abstraction in all aspects of our lives. Whether devising a groundbreaking software application, training a neural network to understand the nuances of human speech, or grappling with the profound questions of our existence, abstraction remains at the core of our efforts to navigate and understand the complex world we inhabit, informing our successes and driving our curiosity forward into the vast unknown.

## Balancing Simplification with Retaining Essential Details: The Risks and Rewards of Abstraction

As the world becomes increasingly complex, mastering the art of abstraction is essential in simplifying intricate systems and processes, making it possible for us to comprehend, leverage, and exploit the inherent dynamics of the world. However, finding the delicate balance between simplification and retention of essential details can be a challenging task, with potential pitfalls that can lead to oversimplification or obfuscation of critical information.

Let's begin with the story of a software architect leading a team in the development of a cutting-edge artificial intelligence platform. The architect surveys the project's vast scope and decides to use abstraction to divide it into manageable components so that each team member can focus on a specific module. However, in the quest for simplicity, the architect over-abstracts the features and functionality of the platform so that the team members receive overly simplified instructions, ultimately compromising the platform's effectiveness and functionality. In this case, the pursuit of abstraction led to the removal of crucial details necessary for the successful implementation of the project.

On the other hand, imagine a scenario where a corporate strategy team abstracts an organization's diverse portfolio of products into strategic categories, enabling senior management to make better decisions about resource allocation. The team carefully balances the need to simplify the categories with retaining essential information about each product's market dynamics and growth potential. As a result, the senior management can make informed decisions and effectively allocate resources, thus fostering the growth and development of the organization.

Both examples highlight how striking the right balance between simplification and information retention in abstraction is critical in achieving desired outcomes.

When embracing abstraction, understanding the delicate interplay between simplification and retention of essential details is crucial. Too much detail can hinder the broader understanding of the problem, while excessive simplification can distort the true nature of the issue at hand. Thus, skillful practitioners of abstraction must be aware of the risks associated with either extreme and strive for a balance that facilitates effective problem-solving without sacrificing important information.

Striving for balance begins with maintaining a critical awareness of context. As the practitioner, you need to assess which features of a given problem are truly unique and essential and which can be abstracted away to reveal underlying structures, relationships, or processes. An architect, for instance, must retain critical properties of the materials they're working with while skillfully abstracting away less relevant details such as the manufacturing process, color, or branding. Similarly, a computer scientist should discern the core concepts and algorithms behind complex code while simplifying the more superficial or repetitive aspects.

Maintaining the context-specific nature of abstraction is where creativity comes into play. A creative mind can navigate complex systems by coming up with innovative ways to simplify constructs, keeping essential details intact while eschewing the superfluous. A molecular biologist studying the human genome might leverage this creativity to break the intricacies of gene expressions down into broader mechanisms or pathways, focusing on crucial features while abstracting the less relevant aspects.

A useful tip for finding this balance involves using metaphors and analogies. Metaphors can serve as powerful tools for simplification, offering practitioners the means to communicate complex ideas or relationships in terms that are readily understandable by a wider audience. For instance, a neuroscientist might use the metaphor of a symphony orchestra to describe the highly choreographed firing of neurons that governs our thoughts and behavior. However, using metaphors requires careful judgment to ensure that they convey the essential details of the complex concept without becoming misleading.

In conclusion, striking the right balance between simplification and retaining essential details in abstraction is a delicate, yet vital, endeavor in today's ever - evolving complexities. By maintaining an awareness of context, unleashing your creativity, and using metaphors judiciously, you can navigate the multidimensional landscapes of modern challenges with finesse and skill. After all, as painter Piet Mondrian said, "The position of the artist is humble. He is essentially a channel." Let this humble position guide your quest for balance in abstraction, using your mastery of the art as a means to illuminate the essential in a world of overwhelming complexity.

## Developing an Abstraction Mindset: Cultivating the Cognitive Skills to Comprehend Problems at a Higher Level

The power of abstract thinking often becomes evident when we face complex problems that require high levels of cognitive dexterity. Einstein famously said that if he had one hour to solve a problem that threatened the very existence of humanity, he would spend the first 55 minutes understanding and refining the problem, and only the last 5 minutes devising an appropriate solution. Herein lies the art of abstraction: the ability to think beyond the immediate particulars, to sieve through the confusion of myriad details and patterns in order to discern the relevant essence, and ultimately navigate the winding path of purposeful problem - solving.

Imagine a software engineering team embarking on creating an innovative application that will disrupt the market. They are confronted with a wide array of challenges: UI design, backend architecture, performance optimization, security concerns, and so on. One essential skill that this team must possess is the ability to abstract their thinking - to sift through the details of each of these issues and focus on the overarching patterns and structures at play. In this scenario, cultivating an abstraction mindset transcends traditional domain knowledge and technical expertise; it enables the team to approach problems from a higher plane of thought, resulting in more efficient and effective decision - making.

So how does one develop an abstraction mindset? The journey begins with cultivating metacognition, or "thinking about our thinking." By becoming mindful of the way our minds function - how we process information, conceptualize ideas, and solve problems - we can begin to identify areas where we can flex our abstraction muscles. One effective way to hone our metacognitive skills is through the practice of deliberate reflection. For example, upon completing a programming task, one can review the problem - solving process, identifying which aspects of the problem were extraneous and which were crucial in arriving at a solution. By understanding the common patterns that emerge in this reflection, we better ourselves to navigate future challenges with an abstraction - focused mindset.

Another powerful exercise in abstraction is the intentional seeking out of diverse perspectives, as they help reveal patterns and structures that would otherwise remain hidden. Consider the software engineering team again - by crowdsourcing ideas from colleagues with different backgrounds, skill sets, and cognitive styles, they can draw on a rich pool of abstractions to guide their problem - solving efforts. This exercise in cross - pollination applies equally well to individual practitioners, who can benefit from a wide - ranging exploration of adjacent fields and disciplines to foster cognitive flexibility and diversify their abstraction toolkit.

A word of caution, though; abstraction is not a one - size - fits - all process. The complexities of each problem domain and the nuances of individual contexts demand a careful balance between generalization and specificity. Over - abstraction can lead to oversimplification and essential details being lost, while under - abstraction can leave problem solvers mired in the details and unable to progress. The key is to approach each problem with an open mind and a healthy respect for the inherent tensions that exist between simplification and maintaining essential detail.

As with any skill, the development of an abstraction mindset is a lifelong journey. It requires dedication, curiosity, and the ability to learn from both successes and failures. Pursuing mastery in abstraction is no easy feat, but it stands to confer remarkable benefits on those who strive to see the world through the lens of patterns and structures that lie beneath the surface of our everyday reality.

As the evolving landscape of human endeavor encapsulates increasingly intricate problem domains, the need for abstraction-minded individuals will only continue to grow. The transformative power of abstract thinking holds the key to unlocking our ability to discern the essential from the superfluous, recognize the unseen patterns in complex systems, and ultimately redefine our capacity for problem-solving in a world that demands ever-greater levels of cognitive finesse. The onus is upon us to take up the mantle of abstraction, and traverse the uncharted realms of human thought that await our exploration. Venture forth, brave abstract thinkers; never before have the rewards in store been so great, and the need for your unique insights so pressing.

# Chapter 2

# Types of Abstraction: Exploring Functional, Modular, Physical, Recursive, and Temporal Abstraction

In the quest to manage complexity in a world increasingly inundated with information, abstraction offers a powerful mental toolset to discern patterns and structure while discarding the superfluous. Mastering abstraction requires understanding not only its foundational principles but also exploring the distinct types and their unique attributes: functional, modular, physical, recursive, and temporal abstraction.

Functional abstraction simplifies complex processes by encapsulating them within functions that describe their essential behavior. Consider how a software application might handle user authentication. This vital task involves multiple steps, such as collecting credentials, processing submitted data, and invoking server - side actions. However, from an abstract perspective, the entire procedure can be represented as a single function: authenticateUser(userCredentials). Functional abstraction offers an elegant way to capture the essence of a complex process without delving into details, all while making it reusable and adaptable to changes within the process.

In a distinct yet complementary vein, modular abstraction helps manage

complexity by breaking down systems into smaller, manageable components. By compartmentalizing functionality and isolating responsibilities,
modular abstraction furthers the ability to focus on individual pieces in
isolation - a significant advantage in troubleshooting and maintenance. To
illustrate, imagine a distributed and interactive system for managing an
office environment. It can consist of interlocking components, such as a
room scheduler, access control, and user registration. Each can be seen as
an abstract module that cooperates with others to provide a seamless user
experience, creating a harmonious system of interacting subsystems.

The art of abstracting also extends to representing real - world entities,
manifested in the form of physical abstraction. Creating this representation
involves reducing complex systems to their constituent parts, akin to a
machine broken down to gears and levers, stripped from its casing. For
example, consider a task that involves predicting the outcome of a soccer
match. Physical abstraction could involve deconstructing the match into
discrete factors, such as player statistics, weather conditions, and team
histories. In doing so, physical abstraction facilitates modeling, simulation,
and analysis by capturing the salient characteristics of the phenomenon at
hand.

The realm of abstraction, however, does not stop at conceiving entities
or functions discretely. Recursive abstraction sees patterns within patterns,
leveraging the power of repetition, self-similarity, and hierarchy to find structure in complex problems. Fractal geometry, for instance, depicts visually
stunning shapes born out of recursive abstraction, such as the Mandelbrot
set or the Sierpinski triangle. By recognizing these self - replicating patterns,
recursive abstraction illuminates deep - seated structures within the most
intricate of phenomena.

Last but not least, temporal abstraction incorporates the dimension
of time in abstractive thinking. Grasping complex systems with time
- dependent characteristics requires an understanding of their evolution
and interactions over time. By identifying recurring patterns and crucial
moments in temporal sequences, it becomes feasible to process, analyze, and
make informed decisions on time-sensitive data. A compelling demonstration
of temporal abstraction is within the domain of algorithmic trading, where
analyzing financial market trends to inform buy and sell decisions hinges on
the ability to abstract meaningful patterns from noisy, ever - changing data.

In conclusion, the great tapestry of abstraction is composed of threads intertwining and separating, converging and diverging. Functional, modular, physical, recursive, and temporal abstraction each illuminates a unique facet of how we perceive, process, and act on complex information. Fortifying our understanding of these distinct types is essential for wielding abstraction as a potent weapon in the battle against complexity. As we venture further into the realm of abstraction, we embark on a journey to cultivate a holistic mindset that empowers us to manage the ever-growing intricacies of our world.

## Functional Abstraction: Simplifying Complex Processes

Functional abstraction is a powerful mental tool that allows us to distill processes into their most essential components, stripping away the extraneous noise that often threatens to overburden our cognitive capacity. By distilling a process down to its most vital functions, we can better understand, manipulate, and optimize it, making it more efficient and transparent. In the realm of computer science, functional abstraction is as critical as oil in an engine, enabling developers to design algorithms that make the most of limited resources and solve problems otherwise thought impossible.

Consider a traveler at a train station, facing the daunting challenge of navigating an unfamiliar transportation network. At first glance, the various timetables, stations, and routes can be overwhelming. However, if the traveler can abstract the critical components - such as arrival and departure times, transfer points, and final destinations - an otherwise insurmountable task can become more manageable. With functional abstraction, the chaos of the train station can be tamed.

Parallel to the traveler's plight is the challenge faced by computer scientists tackling complex algorithms. Let us dive into the world of graph theory and explore one of the most well-known problems - the traveling salesman problem. Here, the goal is to find the shortest possible route that visits each city exactly once and returns to the origin city. At first glance, the problem appears simple, but its combinatorial nature makes it notoriously difficult to solve. To tackle this issue, functional abstraction serves as a mental scalpel, cutting through the problem's gristle and fat until only the lean, mathematical muscle remains.

By focusing on the core function of an algorithm - aspiring to find the shortest possible route - the computer scientist peels back the layers of complexity inherent to the problem. Recursive functions, dynamic programming techniques, and heuristics contribute to conceiving an optimal solution. By abstracting the problem to its barest form, the programmer can identify the algorithm's core functionalities by testing, iterating, and optimizing its behavior.

While functional abstraction is a powerful analytical tool, it is not without its limitations. The process by which we distill complex processes into their core components depends on our capacity for recognizing what is essential and what can be safely discarded. Fallibility lurks in our ability to accurately identify what is critical and what is superfluous. Some level of detail, context, or information may be lost in the course of abstraction, risking the possibility of designing an algorithm that is suboptimal or fails to address the underlying problem.

To illustrate this point, let us return to the metaphor of the train station. Suppose that the traveler, in an attempt to simplify their understanding of the transportation system, discards vital information, such as the fact that the train schedule operates on a 24 - hour clock. By assuming that trains operate only within daytime hours, the traveler may find themselves stranded without a way to reach their destination. Functional abstraction, while a critical tool in managing complexity, can become a double - edged sword if not wielded judiciously.

Thus, it is vital to strike a balance between reducing complexity and preserving essential information when employing functional abstraction. By carefully discerning which aspects of a complex process are genuinely essential, we can better deploy functional abstraction to understand and optimize our mental models.

In the case of a computer scientist, mastery of functional abstraction requires a keeney understanding of the intricacies of the specific problem domain and experience navigating such puzzles. By coupling functional abstraction with deep domain knowledge, the computer scientist can devise an algorithm that is both elegant and powerful - a masterstroke of analytical prowess. The seemingly infinite possibilities in the world of algorithms become refined, crystallizing into a concise, precise solution that solves the problem at hand.

In summary, functional abstraction allows us to simplify complex processes by focusing on their essential components, enabling us to understand and manipulate them more effectively. However, it is crucial to maintain a keen awareness of the balance between simplification and maintaining vital information, requiring both skill and experience. As we venture into the depths of other abstraction techniques, such as modular abstraction, physical abstraction, and temporal abstraction, we will continue to find that this delicate balance between simplification and information retention remains a critical aspect of abstract thinking. We must refine our scalpel-like precision and reach an even greater understanding, unlocking the doors to the undiscovered territories of abstraction.

## Modular Abstraction: Deconstructing Systems into Manageable Components

As we journey through the realm of abstraction, we shall now explore the enigmatic concept of modular abstraction - a method that embodies the art of breaking down complex systems into manageable, digestible, and reusable components. This may seem like black magic to the uninitiated, but to the ones who embrace this form of abstraction, it is a revelation of logical beauty.

Consider how modular abstraction has revolutionized the world of software engineering. Disparate, monolithic programs have been deconstructed into smaller, task-specific modules that can be combined and reused like Lego blocks. This metamorphosis not only eases our cognitive load when grappling with seemingly impenetrable structures but also invites an impressive degree of flexibility and creativity.

Take, for instance, a popular software framework that helps developers build web applications. Instead of writing an entire application from scratch, developers can draw from a rich variety of pre-built modules that handle common tasks such as user authentication, database management, or request handling. These modules are built to be independent, interconnected, and reusable, striking the perfect balance between orderliness and versatility.

Another vivid illustration of modular abstraction at work can be found in the realm of product development, where the concept itself transcends beyond the confines of software engineering. Picture a modern automobile, its many intricate subsystems working in harmony to create a comfortable, efficient, and safe driving experience. The brilliance of the automotive engineers lies not just in devising individual parts such as the engine or the brakes but also in their intricate assembly into a congruous whole.

Now, let us pause to reflect on the merits and imperfections of modular abstraction. In its most virtuous form, it cuts through the Gordian knot of complexity by subdividing a colossal problem into smaller puzzles, analogous to how a sculptor carefully chisels a masterpiece from an unyielding block of stone. However, without a discerning approach and vigilance against unintended consequences, the very act of carving out these modules can result in anarchy - a forest of toolboxes in disarray, with redundant, convoluted, or ill-structured components.

Moving forward, we shall delve into a case study on the implementation of modular abstraction in developing a software system for a transportation company. A once monolithic and unwieldy system was intelligently fragmented into distinct modules, each responsible for vital functions such as vehicle management, route planning, or tracking driver performance. To ensure seamless communication and coordination among these various cogwheels, clearly defined interfaces and contracts were etched into each module's blueprint. Consequently, this renaissance in modularity empowered the company to create new features or optimize existing ones swiftly and with minimal disruption, a feat unattainable in its previous incarnation.

## Physical Abstraction: Representing Real-World Entities in Abstract Terms

To begin, let us consider the humble city map. With its clean lines and simple symbols, a city map captures the essential structures of urban spaces, enabling us to navigate the intricate labyrinth of streets and landmarks with ease. The map's greatest strength, however, is not its representational fidelity, but its selective omission of irrelevant information. The map does not bother with the minutiae of building facades, street lamps, or trees; instead, it presents us with an abstract representation that retains the most important elements needed for navigation. In doing so, the map demonstrates the power of physical abstraction to transform unwieldy, complex systems into manageable, comprehensible structures.

Now, imagine applying this same process of abstraction to a different arena: the automotive industry. The design and manufacture of modern cars require the integration of thousands of individual components, each with its own properties and behaviors. Physical abstraction allows us to represent these components as abstract entities, with clearly defined interfaces and simplified behavior models. For instance, let us consider the functioning of a car's braking system. Instead of having to understand the intricate mechanical details of the various components involved - a potentially overwhelming task - we can represent the system in terms of abstract entities, such as the brake pedal, brake pads, and braking force. This higher - level representation allows us to reason about the braking system's overall behavior and design more effectively, without getting lost in the minutiae of individual parts.

The power of physical abstraction is not limited to simplifying individual systems or components; when harnessed by disciplines such as simulation and data science, it also enables us to understand the dynamic interplay between systems and their governing principles. Consider, for example, the challenge of modeling the Earth's climate. The Earth's climate is an incredibly complex, nonlinear system that arises from the interactions between the atmosphere, land, and ocean. To develop accurate and informative climate models, scientists must first abstract away unnecessary details from these various components - such as the specific terrain of mountain ranges, the precise chemical composition of the atmosphere, or the temperature profiles of individual ocean currents - and focus instead on capturing the essential processes that govern their behavior.

We see striking examples of successful physical abstraction at work in the world of neural networks and deep learning. Here, the complex patterns and high - dimensional datasets often defy human understanding, challenging us to develop meaningful abstractions that can inform both algorithm design and decision - making. One powerful example of this is in the use of deep learning techniques for facial recognition. By representing an individual's face in terms of abstract features such as edges and textures, deep learning systems can achieve remarkable levels of accuracy and robustness to variation in lighting, pose, and expression.

However, with great power comes great responsibility. As enticing as physical abstraction may be in simplifying complex systems and processes, it also carries the potential for harm when applied indiscriminately or without sufficient regard for the underlying realities. The pitfalls of abstraction can manifest in various forms, such as the loss of critical information, unintended consequences, or oversimplification that leads to poor decision-making. For example, suppose a city planner were to design a new public transportation system based on an abstracted representation of the city's street network that omits information about topography and population distribution. In that case, the resulting system might prove wholly inadequate for the city's actual needs, leading to wasted resources and public discontent.

The key to avoiding such pitfalls lies in recognizing the limits of physical abstraction and developing the nuanced thinking needed to navigate its inherent trade-offs. This requires a deep understanding of the systems being abstracted, a willingness to question assumptions and revisit earlier decisions, and the ability to recognize when and where essential details must be retained. By cultivating these skills and approaching abstraction with a critical, discerning eye, we can harness its power to address the complexity of our world while avoiding the snares that it can at times beget.

As we continue to engage with and explore the myriad ways abstraction can enrich our understanding and problem-solving capabilities, let us not forget the lessons learned from our journey into the realm of physical abstraction. The immense value of abstraction, tempered by the need for caution and critical thinking, will guide us as we tackle the promises and challenges of other types of abstraction, extending our understanding of the unifying power of simplification and generalization.

## Recursive and Temporal Abstraction: Leveraging Patterns and Time in Problem Solving

In the dynamic world of problem-solving, the ability to detect patterns and understand the inherent structure beneath complex systems can open doors to innovative thinking and groundbreaking solutions. Faced with mysteries hidden beneath layers of intricate data and interactions, our quest for understanding is often best supported by two powerful techniques: recursive abstraction and temporal abstraction. Both strategies offer essential keys to unlocking the power of patterns and time, leading to more efficient, elegant, and effective problem-solving across diverse fields and applications.

Recursive abstraction is a technique that reveals the underlying structure of problems by breaking them into smaller, similar subproblems. Recursive abstraction relies on the fact that, in many cases, a complex problem can be divided into multiple smaller, more manageable problems with a similar structure that can be solved independently. The solutions to these subproblems can then be recombined, ultimately unraveling the original complexity and paving a way to the overall solution. Recursive abstraction is an invaluable method found in various disciplines, from mathematics and computer science to socio-economic studies and environmental research.

Consider the well-known problem of traversing a labyrinth, often depicted as a winding path with multiple dead-ends designed to trap the unwary traveler. A recursive abstraction approach to solving this problem requires breaking down the labyrinth into smaller, similar mazes that can be tackled individually. With every successful traversal, the individual maze solutions provide insights into a broader understanding of the overall labyrinth structure. By combining these insights, the path through the labyrinth is gradually revealed.

Temporal abstraction, on the other hand, focuses on understanding change and dynamics across time. This technique is employed to identify patterns and interactions within time-based data and often involves the simplification and representation of intricate dynamics using abstract temporal structures. Temporal abstraction enables the systematic exploration of both short-term and long-term trends, leading to deeper insights and better decision-making. Detecting these temporal patterns can reveal hidden connections and dependencies between events, enabling a more comprehensive understanding of complex interactions across various fields, including finance, healthcare, and natural sciences.

For example, imagine analyzing the spread of a viral disease through a population. Employing temporal abstraction would involve examining the patterns of infection over time, identifying how the contagion spreads through various demographics, and recognizing underlying factors influencing the spread. By detecting the temporal patterns, public health officials can adapt interventions with precision and efficiency, mitigating the impact on the population and reducing both morbidity and mortality rates.

The beauty of recursive and temporal abstraction lies in their complementary nature. Combining these approaches can create even more powerful solutions for time - based, structured problems. Take, for instance, the analysis of a vast financial dataset of stock prices across different industries and time periods. Recursive abstraction could be employed to break down the problem into clusters of similar companies, while temporal abstraction would reveal trends and seasonality within these subgroups. The synergy of these approaches allows deeper understanding and more accurate predictions of market trends, helping decision - makers plan their investments with greater confidence.

No technique is without its challenges, and recursive and temporal abstraction are no exception. Both methods require discerning the appropriate level of detail in breaking down problems, ensuring that neither excessive simplification nor overcomplication obscures the solution. However, when used wisely, recursive and temporal abstraction can truly enhance our capacity to tackle some of the most complex problems the world has to offer.

As our journey through problem - solving continues, the virtues of abstraction are not exclusive to complexity and time. Equipped with an ever - growing toolbox of abstraction techniques, we must venture forth with a fervent curiosity, an open mind, and the humility to recognize the intricacy and fragility of the world. In doing so, we stand to unravel the secrets of complex systems, derive valuable insights at every level of abstraction, and harness the full potential of our collective creativity and ingenuity.

# Chapter 3

# Applying Abstraction in Real - world Problems: Case Studies in Software Architecture, Product Development, and Strategic Planning

In software architecture, abstraction allows engineers to simplify the complexity of computing systems by dividing them into smaller, manageable components. Consider the classic example of designing a database system. Database architects must create tables, enumerate associations between them, and establish the sequence of transactions. By defining these components by their essential properties - simplicity, flexibility, and portability - architects can describe the system using a more concise and coherent language. The resulting abstractions facilitate communication among team members and help align their ideas in a more structured and productive environment.

Another software - related case involves a highly - competitive gaming application. In this scenario, the development team aims to develop a robust and scalable platform capable of hosting millions of online players. Here, abstraction manifests in the form of modularization and functional decomposition. Instead of tackling the entire, intricate system at once, developers use abstraction to break it down into smaller, interconnected modules: game engine, user interface, matchmaking, and player authentication. Focusing on these distinct modules allows the team to iteratively improve the platform with each refined abstraction leading to a better version of the software.

Similarly, in product development, abstraction proves invaluable in bringing innovative ideas to market. Let's take the case of a company that decides to launch a new fitness product. The design team recognizes the need to elegantly integrate a multitude of features - activity tracking, sleep monitoring, user engagement, among others - into a sleek device. By employing physical and temporal abstraction, the team decouples the hardware design from the software and considers various materials and manufacturing processes. Furthermore, they examine usage patterns and expectations, as well as user feedback, to iterate on subsequent prototypes. The iterative use of abstraction in product development ultimately leads to the creation of a successful fitness device, resonating with consumers and capturing market share.

In strategic planning, abstraction proves pivotal in articulating long - term objectives and projecting hypothetical scenarios. For instance, a large telecommunications firm might confront a future fraught with uncertainties - technology disruptions, shifting regulations, and competitive pressures. By leveraging recursive abstraction, the firm's executives can analyze the industry landscape, unraveling deeper insights into the ongoing intricacies of the industry. In doing so, they can conceptualize viable pathways into the future and apply these patterns to the overarching strategy. With each successive abstraction, the company derives greater clarity on its priorities and resources, optimizing its competitive position over time.

Moreover, these executives could employ temporal abstraction to forecast the company's performance. They might assemble past financial data into meaningful trends and extrapolate these trends into various "threads of time" representing potential outcomes. Such abstraction allows decision - makers to better apprehend the dynamics, risks, and opportunities at their disposal. Consequently, they gain the confidence and foresight needed to navigate an uncertain world.

These case studies elucidate the power and adaptability of abstraction across various domains. From systemizing software components to envisioning possible futures, abstraction serves as an indispensable thinking tool, translating intricate realities into simpler, clearer representations. By discarding irrelevant details and identifying shared structures, we can harvest the essence of the problems we face and foster new solutions with unparalleled creativity. That said, abstraction is a double-edged sword - overuse or misuse may lead to oversimplification, loss of nuance, or even ethical dilemmas. As we continue our exploration into abstraction, we must remain mindful of keeping our abstractions grounded and harmonized with their contexts in order to ensure responsible and effective problem-solving.

## Software Architecture: Implementing Modular and Functional Abstraction

Software architecture lies at the heart of designing and implementing complex systems. It provides a blueprint for organizing functionality, managing dependencies, and ensuring performance, scalability, and maintainability. To achieve these goals, architects rely heavily on two cornerstone abstraction techniques: modular abstraction and functional abstraction. These methods offer powerful strategies for taming complexity and creating software that is robust, adaptable, and efficient.

Modular abstraction is premised on the decomposition of a system into its constituent components. These encapsulated modules are designed to be highly cohesive - that is, they have a well-defined and singular focus - and loosely coupled, meaning they depend as little as possible on each other to function correctly. This decomposition allows for easier comprehension, more effective maintenance, and better extensibility of the software, while also promoting a separation of concerns that is crucial for managing complexity.

Consider the construction of a modern web application, for instance. Its components might consist of user interfaces, business logic, and data storage subsystems. By breaking down the system into these discrete components, architects can focus on the design and implementation of each module separately, without being overwhelmed by the intricate details of the entire application. This enables them to make informed decisions in crafting specialized interfaces, reducing dependencies, and allowing each piece to evolve independently and even be replaced entirely without causing major disruptions to the whole system.

Meanwhile, functional abstraction operates on a finer scale, concentrating on the behavior of individual components. By treating functions as reusable, abstract entities, programmers can design and implement complex behavior without wading through the intricacies of low-level representation. This approach minimizes redundancy and promotes clarity, simplification, and reusability across the system.

An illustrative example of functional abstraction can be found in the functional programming paradigm, where pure functions take center stage as the primary means of solving problems. By treating functions as first-class citizens, this approach harnesses the power of abstraction to build software using composable building blocks. Functions are defined with a clear contract that specifies their outputs based solely on their inputs. A sortBy function, for example, might be crafted to receive a list of objects and a comparator function, returning a sorted list based on the comparator's logic without altering the original list. This sortBy function can be reused across numerous scenarios, as its abstraction allows it to operate independently of the specific data types or structures it is applied to.

The interplay of modular and functional abstraction in software architecture is rich and fertile, enabling the creation of sophisticated systems that are manageable, maintainable, and scalable. The success of the Unix operating system, for instance, is often attributed to its adhesion to modular and functional design principles. Unix embodies the "small pieces, loosely joined" philosophy, allowing it to evolve into one of the most flexible, adaptable, and robust systems the world has seen.

Yet, achieving the desired balance and fluidity between these abstractions requires careful contemplation and expertise. It is not uncommon to witness the pitfalls of over-abstracting, where excessive generalization takes a toll on performance or usability, or to suffer from the brittleness induced by the heavy coupling of seemingly independent modules. By learning from the successes and failures of numerous projects, architects can hone their abilities to identify the appropriate levels of abstraction, navigating intricate scenarios with grace and acumen.

Harnessing the power of modular and functional abstraction is a vital aspect of mastering the art of software design. With proficiency, architects can transcend low-level details and build grand, elaborate systems that elegantly cater to the ever-evolving needs of users. As we traverse further

into the vast landscape of abstraction, we shall uncover how these principles
can be applied in tandem with other techniques to invigorate not only
the design and construction of software but also the realm of product
development, strategic planning, and problem-solving at large.

## Product Development: Leveraging Temporal and Physical Abstraction for Efficient Design

Product development is an intricate and often demanding process that
involves the careful orchestration of resources, time, and creativity. In
today's fast-paced market, being able to leverage abstraction techniques
can not only make the process more efficient but also lead to innovative and
unique product offerings. Specifically, temporal and physical abstraction
techniques can be employed to streamline the product development process,
ensuring that teams can maintain their competitive edge and create products
that truly stand out among the competition.

One of the key aspects of product development is creating detailed
design specifications and requirements. These specifications serve as the
blueprint for every aspect of the product's development and are pivotal in
addressing customer needs, as well as ensuring a seamless integration of the
various components that make up the final product. By employing temporal
abstraction techniques, product development teams can break down complex
design requirements into simpler time-based segments, allowing for a more
manageable development process.

To illustrate the power of temporal abstraction, consider a company
developing a cutting-edge smartwatch. By focusing on specific time-based
milestones, such as particular functions needed by users in the morning, the
afternoon, or the evening, the design process can be significantly streamlined.
For example, designing functions for the morning timeframe could include
features such as a gentle alarm, morning exercise tracking, and calendar
reminders for the day. By breaking the product's features and functionality
into smaller time-bound segments, designers and engineers can focus on one
aspect of the smartwatch at a time, knowing that each segment is a crucial
piece of the larger puzzle. This abstraction technique not only enables teams
to deliver products that cater to a user's needs at specific times, but it also
makes the process more efficient and organized.

Physical abstraction techniques, on the other hand, boil down the complex real-world entities and objects into simpler, more manageable representations of their essential characteristics. This allows product development teams to iterate on the product's design more efficiently while ensuring that each component complies with the overarching design specifications. For instance, imagine a team designing a drone for professional film-making. The drone must be able to carry a high-quality camera, navigate through diverse environments, and have enough battery capacity for extended flights - all while adhering to specific weight and size constraints.

By employing physical abstraction techniques, the team can create abstract models of each component (e.g., the drone's frame, motors, propellers, and battery) to evaluate their individual performance and compatibility with the overall design. By simulating the interaction of these abstract models, engineers can quickly identify potential issues, make necessary adjustments, and refine the product's design without investing excessive resources in prototyping and testing for every iteration. This abstraction-based approach not only saves precious time and resources but significantly improves the overall product development efficiency.

In the realm of product development, temporal and physical abstraction techniques can also be combined to create even more efficient design processes. For instance, a project's timeline can be broken down into smaller development stages, where each stage focuses on the integration and testing of specific components or subsystems. This approach ensures that each part of the product undergoes rigorous evaluation and refinement in a systematic and organized manner, ultimately resulting in a final product that is both innovative and reliable.

As the market becomes increasingly saturated and competitive, the need for efficient and inventive product development processes is greater than ever. In this context, temporal and physical abstraction techniques offer invaluable tools for fostering creativity, reducing complexity, and ultimately driving innovation. Armed with these techniques and the mindset to wield them effectively, product development teams can rise to the challenge of creating groundbreaking products that not only stand out in the market but truly cater to the evolving needs and desires of the customer.

## Strategic Planning: Recursive Abstraction and Scenario Analysis

As we journey into the world of strategic planning, we must find an efficient and effective way to navigate the complex, interwoven landscape of possible scenarios and outcomes. In this sea of information and potential ramifications, how does one stay afloat while keeping an eye on the horizon for potential threats and opportunities? The answer lies in the powerful, yet often misunderstood, art of recursive abstraction and scenario analysis.

To illuminate the intricacies of recursive abstraction, consider a game of chess. Faced with a complex, multi-tiered chessboard with countless possible moves and outcomes, a highly skilled chess player can assess the board by grouping multiple steps and levels of consequences into a single unit of analysis. They can identify patterns and rippling effects that extend through time, allowing them not only to plan their immediate move but also to anticipate the consequences of each choice, foresee roadblocks, and adapt their strategy along the way. This holistic habit of mind is what characterizes recursive abstraction - breaking down a complex problem by working backward from end goals, prioritizing actions based on the culmination of potential scenarios, and continuously updating the analysis based on new information.

Scenario analysis complements recursive abstraction by exploring the various "what-if" scenarios and probabilistic outcomes associated with a given decision or strategic direction. It is a systematic approach to examining the potential consequences of a choice by testing key assumptions within different future possibilities. Instead of focusing solely on traditional forecasting methods, scenario analysis seeks to challenge and enrich our understanding of how a particular decision might unfold in different future contexts.

Now, let us examine the practical application of recursive abstraction and scenario analysis in strategic planning. Picture a startup company developing an innovative electric vehicle (EV). The management team is faced with numerous decisions ranging from financing, marketing, product development, and supply chain management. The complexity is overwhelming, and making a decision requires navigating a labyrinth of potential outcomes and consequences. Utilizing recursive abstraction, the team begins by identifying their ultimate, desired outcome - for example, establishing a sustainable, market-leading EV company that generates significant profits and positively impacts society and the environment.

Armed with a clear end goal, the startup begins to work backward from this desired outcome to identify the various milestones, roadblocks, and actions that might be required to achieve such a future. Through the lens of recursive abstraction, the interconnected nature of the strategic plan emerges as decisions about financing, marketing, product development, and supply chain management become intertwined with one another.

Next, the startup integrates scenario analysis to develop and explore different "what-if" cases that could impact their recursive strategic plan. Using these scenarios, they can stress-test their strategic decisions under various assumptions, such as the regulatory environment for EVs, customer adoption rates, or even unforeseeable crises such as a global pandemic. By challenging their assumptions and exploring the resilience of their strategic plan across these scenarios, the startup gains valuable insights that ensure adaptive, robust decision-making.

Taking our EV startup example further, the management may identify four distinct strategic pathways influenced by two key uncertainties; the pace of technological innovation and the adoption of sustainable energy policies in major markets. By crafting four alternative future scenarios that explore these uncertainties, the management team can better understand the implications and consequences of their strategic choices within each narrative, and make more informed decisions that set the company on the best path to achieving their desired future.

As we traverse the intricate world of strategic planning, recursive abstraction and scenario analysis provide a compass and guiding star, allowing us to navigate the complexities and uncertainties with greater clarity, intention, and adaptability. By combining these methods, we can create comprehensive, adaptive strategic plans that are better prepared to face the inevitable twists and turns that await us on our journey towards our ideal future state.

In the intricate dance of decision-making that is strategic planning, let us not be daunted by complexity, nor cling blindly to the familiar and predictable. Instead, let us embrace the powerful techniques of recursive abstraction and scenario analysis to craft adaptive strategies that acknowledge the web of interconnected actions, consequences, and scenarios. And as we chart our own paths towards a flourishing future, may we remember the wise words of legendary chess grandmaster Garry Kasparov: "There is no greater moment in life than the instant your opponent hesitates, and you know you have him." Let our mastery of abstraction and scenario analysis serve as our shields and weapons, empowering us to seize those decisive moments and overcome the boundless challenges before us.

## Case Study: Applying Multiple Abstraction Techniques in the Development of an AI - Based Solution

Imagine an ambitious start - up setting out to develop an AI - based solution aimed at diagnosing early - stage diseases through the analysis of medical imaging data. To achieve this goal, the development team needed to consider an array of abstraction techniques at their disposal, ranging from functional to recursive abstraction, in order to create a cohesive and scalable system that could interpret complex medical data and produce reliable diagnoses.

First, the team employed functional abstraction to simplify the complex processes involved in the analysis of vast amounts of medical image data. By breaking down these processes into smaller, manageable functions, such as image pre - processing, feature extraction, classification, and interpretation, the solution could specialize in each stage and achieve high precision in its overall analysis.

As the AI solution began to take shape, modular abstraction enabled the team to break down the overall structure into individual components, making it feasible to update specific parts without disrupting the entire system. This modularity allowed developers to work on separate subsystems, such as the feature extraction and classification algorithms, simultaneously. The resulting modular structure also meant that if new techniques or diagnostic criteria arose, they could replace or supplement existing modules without disrupting other parts of the solution.

The careful application of physical abstraction played a pivotal role in representing the real - world entities, such as anatomical structures and pathological features, in abstract terms suitable for machine learning analysis. This translation allowed the AI to make sense of the wealth of medical data it was intended to process.

The team further leveraged recursive abstraction in the training of their AI solution. By iterating on smaller subproblems in medical image analysis, such as identifying key patterns in the data, they generated a model capable of piecing together the "bigger picture" and drawing upon these recursive insights to recognize vital clinical symptoms. Additionally, temporal abstraction allowed this AI to track changes, trends, and anomalies in patient data over time and understand the progression of a disease.

As the AI solution developed, it became crucial to balance simplification with the retention of essential details. If too much information was discarded in the abstraction process, the system could potentially miss subtle but critical clues necessary for accurate diagnosis. By carefully calibrating the level of detail retained in the feature extraction and classification components, the team could achieve both efficiency and precision in their AI system.

The development of the AI - based solution did not progress without significant challenges. The team found themselves wrestling with context - dependence and the need for nuanced thinking in abstraction. For instance, the fluid nature of medical knowledge, with diagnostic criteria and classifications regularly revised, required adaptive methods that could integrate changing definitions and maintain a high standard of interpretation.

Ultimately, the start - up successfully applied a range of abstraction techniques to build an AI - based medical diagnostic tool capable of recognizing early - stage diseases from imaging data. As the solution entered the market and achieved promising results, the team continued to evaluate, refine and learn from their experience in employing abstraction techniques.

## Case Study: Reinventing Organizational Structure through Abstraction and Strategic Planning

The art of abstraction, combined with strategic planning, can be a powerful force in reinventing an organizational structure. Companies that have recognized the need for change and embraced this approach have often found unprecedented success. Our case study of a multinational corporation that recently underwent a bold organizational transformation serves as an insightful example of these principles at work.

The corporation, a well-known conglomerate with operations in multiple industries, had been struggling to adapt in the rapidly changing environment of the digital age. Their structure had become cumbersome, slow to react,

and lacking cohesion across various divisions. Top leadership realized they
needed a new approach that would allow them to respond effectively to new
market entrants, novel threats, and evolving consumer demands. To that
end, they enlisted the help of outside experts and a dedicated internal team
to undertake a comprehensive restructuring effort.

Utilizing abstraction as a core technique, the team began by mapping
out the shared structures and common functions throughout the existing
organization. They focused on discarding superfluous details and uncovering
the elements that tied different departments together. By taking a step back
and viewing the organization from a higher level, they were better equipped
to comprehend problems in the context of the entire company rather than a
particular department.

Functional abstraction played a crucial role in this process, allowing
the team to isolate and understand the complex processes essential to the
corporation's success. They identified key functions such as innovation,
supply chain management, and marketing, and aimed at designing an
organization that would streamline these processes and minimize friction
between them.

Simultaneously, the team sought to implement modular abstraction by
breaking down the existing organization into manageable components that
could be reassembled in a more efficient and cohesive structure. The new
organizational map would consist of interconnected modules representing the
various functions they had identified earlier. These modules would maintain
a certain level of autonomy, allowing each to optimize their performance
and adapt quickly to new challenges.

Temporal abstraction also played a role in the restructuring effort,
particularly in forecasting and strategic planning. By evaluating past
performance and utilizing time - series data, the team was able to make
predictions about future trends and incorporate them into their restructuring
plan. Furthermore, the new organization was designed to be more adaptive,
able to respond and evolve over time as trends changed and new challenges
emerged.

The final result of the restructuring was a dramatically altered organizational chart, with a flatter hierarchy, more interconnected divisions, and
greater emphasis on innovation and customer focus. Functions that were
previously scattered across various departments were now grouped together

in clearly defined modules, allowing for streamlined processes and improved internal alignment.

Upon implementation, the reinvented structure had immediate and profound effects on the company's operations. Amid the seemingly chaotic transformation, employees began to thrive in their newfound autonomy and interconnectivity. Information and ideas flowed between departments more freely, fostering an atmosphere of creativity and collaboration that had been sorely lacking. In addition, flexible modules allowed the organization to respond more rapidly to emergent trends and market changes.

Critics of the restructuring effort may argue that so radical a change could cause disruptions and disorientation for employees. However, by utilizing abstraction as a guiding force, the team managed to smooth out the transition process by focusing on shared structures and common objectives. Additionally, as employees experienced the advantages of the new structure firsthand and witnessed the company's newfound nimbleness, they grew increasingly supportive of the transformation.

In conclusion, our case study demonstrates the transformative power of abstraction when applied to organizational structures. By distilling complex systems into manageable and adaptable components, businesses can evolve and thrive in a world of constant change. As our multinational corporation example vividly shows, bolting on an abstraction mindset to strategic planning gave employees a newfound sense of purpose, reinforced interdepartmental cohesion, and unlocked newfound potential for continued growth and success. As the world shows no sign of slowing down or simplifying, achieving mastery in abstraction-driven restructuring is becoming an indispensable skill for any forward-thinking leader.

## Case Study: Abstraction in Complex Systems - A Tale of Supply Chain Management

The Tale of Supply Chain Management: Abstraction in Complex Systems

Once upon a time, in the vast and interconnected realm of global commerce, there stood a grand empire - the kingdom of Supply Chain Management. Its labyrinthine webs of transportation, transactions, and communications allowed goods to flow across great distances, from the factories of far-eastern lands to the markets of the west. Among its primary concerns were optimizing the flow of goods, maximizing efficiency, and minimizing costs. The kingdom was heralded for its steadfast success in these pursuits, largely through its mastery of abstraction - an art that allowed it to successfully manage complexity in a complex world.

Within the empire, many smaller dominions held unique roles in maintaining the integrity and prosperity of the supply chain. For example, there was the principality of Inventory Management, tasked with maintaining adequate stock levels, and the neighboring duchy of Demand Forecasting, entrusted to predict the fluctuating appetites of the market. Elusive and intricate mechanisms connected these domains in a dance full of nuance, driven by the need to ensure supply met demand.

One remarkable example of abstraction in the kingdom took place in the central citadel of Planning and Coordination, where formidable archivists and scholars labored to create simplified representations of the vast, interconnected machinery that drove the supply chain. Through the use of modular abstraction, the scholars could deconstruct this colossal system into manageable components, each representing specific functions, such as warehousing, transportation, and manufacturing processes. By focusing on the high-level interactions of these modules, decision-makers could easily understand the mechanics of the kingdom and make informed choices without being hindered by the noise of excessive detail.

For instance, to understand the impact of a surge in demand, the scholars would visualize how it affected every part of the supply chain - from procurement to assembly to distribution. By using the modular abstraction, decision-makers in the top echelons of the kingdom could quickly discern which areas required intervention - be it the opening of new factories or the hiring of additional logistics staff - to thwart an impending crisis.

However, the kingdom's preeminent scholars understood that oversimplification through excessive abstraction could obscure valuable insights. Adept in the art of nuance, they carefully discerned which details were essential to retain and which could be cast aside without introducing risk or misrepresentation. Experts in physical abstraction, they were capable of modeling real-world entities such as warehouses, factories, and distribution centers, as simplified components within their overarching supply chain system. Retaining the essential details of these entities while abstracting their intricacies resulted in a model on which the kingdom could base its decisions without falling into the trap of overgeneralization.

In a daring foray into the realm of time, the domain of Temporal Abstraction was established to contend with ever-evolving market conditions. Here, the scholars worked to understand seasonal patterns and trends, using time series data and rolling windows method to refine their forecasts more accurately. By employing temporal abstractions, the kingdom was better equipped to anticipate, adapt, and overcome the challenges wrought by the capriciousness of the global market.

As is the custom in any engrossing tale, the empire also faced looming obstacles that threatened to undermine its foundations. Much like the mythical hydra, cognitive biases seem to sprout new heads just as swiftly as they were excised, leading the kingdom's scholars to implement continuous reflection and improvement in their methodological arsenal. They explored bias in abstraction, diligently mitigating its presence in decision-making processes while integrating inclusivity, diversity, and ethical considerations in their treatments of abstracted models.

Alas, the glorious kingdom of Supply Chain Management thrives in an incessant cycle of collaboration, iteration, abstraction, and refinement. Its ongoing success offers a compelling case study from which other domains can glean valuable lessons to sharpen their ability to wield abstraction in managing complexity with finesse.

And so, with a waft of its magnificent cape, Supply Chain Management strides ahead, undaunted by the enigmas of globalization, buoyed by its mastery of the art of abstraction. In our next chronicle, we shall venture into a realm where technology and intellect meld in harmony: the development of AI-based solutions, where diverse abstraction techniques intermingle to yield a promising and transformative tomorrow.

## Lessons Learned and Best Practices in Applying Abstraction Across Fields

Firstly, it is essential to recognize the context in which abstraction is being employed. This understanding facilitates the appropriate selection of techniques and levels of abstraction for each specific domain. For example, in software engineering, modular and functional abstraction helps manage the complexity of large software systems by breaking them into smaller parts and focusing on their functionality without diving into implementation details. However, applying this approach to strategic planning might result in an oversimplified view that fails to account for environmental factors and interaction dynamics.

A significant lesson to take from these cases is the value of an iterative process in refining abstraction techniques. Through feedback and evaluation, practitioners can continuously improve their methods, striving to strike the appropriate balance between simplification and the preservation of essential information. This iterative approach is critical to managing changing conditions and contexts, ensuring that the chosen level of abstraction remains relevant and effective over time.

From the field of data science, we learn the importance of selecting the right granularity when abstracting. Data models and representations often involve trade - offs between simplicity and the preservation of information, a balance which largely depends on purpose and context. For example, aggregated data may be fitting for high - level summaries but may lose crucial details required for nuanced decision - making. Implementing careful selection processes for features or dimensions in a dataset can circumvent the risk that important information will be lost in the abstraction process. Further, applying multiple levels of abstraction for different analytical tasks enables more comprehensive insights and a deeper understanding of the underlying data patterns.

Turning our gaze to product development, one of the key lessons learned is the power of integrating abstraction techniques throughout the entire product lifecycle. From ideation to development and user testing, abstraction affords opportunities to identify essential features, streamline workflows, and even delve into higher - level discussions around design trade - offs. Throughout these stages, embracing the challenge to question assumptions, recognize personal biases, and explicitly address these factors in the abstraction process culminates in a balanced and more inclusive result.

The case of strategic planning reveals the necessity of avoiding false dichotomies and oversimplification when employing abstraction. In this field, abstraction techniques can provide a concise roadmap for decision - making under uncertainty. However, succumbing to false dichotomies can limit strategic options and constrain the exploration of alternative pathways. It is thus essential to be vigilant in identifying and disentangling false dichotomies, as well as encouraging open - mindedness in the deliberative process.

To successfully apply abstraction across fields, a few general principles emerge as vital. Building a strong foundation of knowledge in the specific domain is indispensable, as expertise allows the discerning of critical information from noise. Additionally, being agile and adapting abstraction techniques to the changing contexts and conditions is crucial, as is fostering an inclusive mindset that accounts for diverse perspectives and avoids potential biases.

By drawing on these lessons and best practices across various fields, professionals can develop a robust and versatile approach to abstraction, employing the technique in powerful and nuanced ways tailored to the unique challenges of their domain. By cultivating this artful balance, practitioners can elevate their decision - making and problem - solving capabilities and help navigate the complexities of an increasingly interconnected world.

# Chapter 4

# The Art of Nuance: Context - Dependence, Higher - Level Reversal, and Attraction to Definitions in Abstract Thinking

In the realm of abstract thinking, nuances often dictate the difference between a profound insight and a shallow generalization. To navigate the intricacies of this art form, one must be attuned to context - dependence, higher - level reversal, and the attraction to definitions. By delving into these aspects, we can elevate our abstract thinking capabilities and improve our overall cognitive prowess in problem - solving and decision - making. To illustrate this further, let us explore relevant examples and applications from various domains.

Context - Dependence in Abstract Thinking

In attempting to optimize a software application's performance, an engineer might intuitively apply the well - known principle of caching - storing frequently - used data in a readily accessible location to reduce computing time. However, this heuristic can be counterproductive if the data access pattern is unpredictable or when the memory overhead outweighs its benefits.

When presented with a different context, a more nuanced understanding of caching would involve a trade - off analysis between time and space complexity. Thus, comprehending the importance of context - dependence may serve as an indispensable tool in selecting the appropriate abstraction for a given problem, transcending the bounds of habitual and simplistic thought patterns.

Higher - Level Reversal: A Tale of Deep Learning

Artificial intelligence has undergone a paradigm shift from rule - based expert systems to data-driven models, exemplifying the notion of higher-level reversal in abstract thinking. Deep learning - a subset of machine learning - discards explicit programming in favor of artificial neural networks that can learn complex patterns from large quantities of data. The counterintuitive nature of this approach led to profound advancements in diverse fields like computer vision, natural language processing, and reinforcement learning. Higher - level reversal teaches us to embrace alternative abstractions when limitations become evident in our current ones. We can apply this mindset across a wide array of disciplines, always keeping a keen eye on the potential for new vantage points.

Attraction to Definitions: Use Cases as a Guiding Star

Abstraction's attraction to definitions concept entails the propensity to gravitate towards clear and concise delineations of complex ideas. When presented with a heterogeneous array of data, an analyst might be tempted to abstract it into categories based on superficial similarities, such as demographic or geographic features.

However, a more nuanced approach demands examining the underlying structure and patterns within the data. For instance, considering customer use cases and segmenting accordingly can unveil otherwise hidden relationships and trends, enabling the development of more tailored strategies. This example showcases the importance of striving towards accurate and meaningful definitions in abstraction, magnetized by the allure of actionable insights and improved decision - making.

As we have illustrated through these varied examples and domains, the art of nuance in abstract thinking is both a challenging and rewarding endeavor. By honing our awareness of context - dependence, higher - level reversal, and attraction to definitions, we elevate our ability to extract the essence of complex problems, casting a discerning gaze upon the ever

- shifting landscape of possibilities. Such intellectual dexterity invites a mindful embrace of uncertainties, paradoxes, and uncharted territories, fueling our endless pursuit of truth and wisdom.

## Understanding Context - Dependence in Abstract Thinking

The art of abstraction is an intellectual dance, an intricate interplay between simplification and detail extraction, that enables us to navigate the complexities of our ever - evolving world. As we engage in higher - level thinking, the ability to identify and extract context is a valuable skill that not only enhances our capacity to grasp intricate concepts but also bolsters our resilience against the pitfalls of overgeneralization and superficial understanding. In essence, understanding context - dependence in abstract thinking is akin to having a keen eye for nuance - a skill that enriches our intellect, fortifies our judgment, and elevates our problem - solving abilities.

Take, for example, the world of computer programming. On the surface, the proliferation of programming languages and frameworks might be mistakenly perceived as a result of technology enthusiasts indulging in their creative whims. However, a keener understanding of context reveals the motivational foundation for their existence. Different programming paradigms cater to specific demands and operational functionalities. For instance, functional programming emphasizes immutability and statelessness, making it ideal for large - scale data processing and parallel computation, whereas object - oriented programming modularizes code and encourages encapsulation of related methods, facilitating software maintenance and extensibility. Being aware of the contextual factors underpinning these abstractions is crucial for discerning the optimal choice in a particular scenario.

The importance of context - dependence in abstraction is further accentuated when we explore architectural design. Imagine an architect faced with the challenge of designing an urban park. Their primary objective would be to devise an abstraction that achieves a harmonious balance between aesthetics, functionality, and sustainability. However, the particularities of the locale, along with its prevailing social, environmental, and economic contexts, would dictate the elements to be negotiated. For example, a city with frequent heavy rainfall necessitates the inclusion of water management features, such as rain gardens and permeable surfaces. Meanwhile, a location with high air pollution levels would benefit from an abundance of air-purifying plants and greenery. Acknowledging these contextual factors ensures that the product of abstraction is not only aesthetically pleasing but also resonates with its surroundings and addresses pressing local issues.

However, the pursuit of context-awareness in abstract thinking is not devoid of challenges. Human beings are wired to prefer shortcuts and heuristics, often curtailing our capacity for engaging in nuanced analysis. Moreover, cognitive biases and emotion-laden evaluations further muddy the landscape of context-dependence. Therefore, nascent abstractions must be approached with a critical and discerning attitude, continuously probing and scrutinizing the interplay of factors shaping them.

One way to enhance context-dependent abstract thinking is by embracing a multidisciplinary approach. By drawing from various fields-how sociology sheds light on human behavior, ecology illuminates the web of life, or game theory unravels strategic decision-making, for example-we prime our brains to consider a kaleidoscope of interconnected factors. This approach fosters a deeper conceptual understanding of the underlying relationships and dependencies, ultimately enabling us to forge refined, relevant, and adaptive abstractions.

Moreover, as we breed context-awareness into our abstraction endeavors, we must finely calibrate our focus between broad generalizations and detailed intricacies. Just as a master painter wields the paintbrush with finesse, knowing when to opt for bold strokes and when to tend to delicate details, a great thinker has a similar command of abstraction, pivoting effortlessly between the fragile grains of context-specificity and the potent unifying themes that pervade human knowledge and experience.

In the ever-evolving tapestry of human thought, understanding context-dependence in abstraction is akin to identifying the intricate yet distinct threads that weave life's complexities into intelligible patterns. As we nurture this ability, we shall find ourselves capable of navigating intricate challenges with confidence and grace, forging solutions that thoughtfully harness the power of abstraction while remaining profoundly cognizant of the unique realities in which our creations must operate. With this awareness comes an invitation to embrace the paradoxes and uncertainties inherent in our world, enabling our abstract thinking to flourish as we chart our course through the fascinating labyrinth that is the human experience.

## Diving into Higher-Level Reversal: Differences between Computer Science and Deep Learning

As we dive into the remarkable world of abstraction, we encounter a curious phenomenon known as higher-level reversal, which can have significant implications for the way we think and solve complex problems. In exploring this idea, let's first examine its manifestation in computer science, and compare it to its counterpart in deep learning.

In computer science, abstraction is a widely-practiced principle that allows us to manage complexity by hiding low-level details and focusing on high-level patterns. This is achieved mainly through functional and modular abstraction techniques, which enable us to design, implement, and maintain sophisticated and large-scale systems. Computing machines, at their core, rely on simple logic gates and binary mathematics to execute even the most intricate functions. However, it would be remarkably challenging to develop complex applications, such as operating systems, databases, and graphical applications, by merely manipulating individual bits and gates.

Higher-level reversal in computer science occurs when the process of abstraction exposes new insights, simplifications, or optimizations that are not apparent at the lower levels of the system. When building a performance-critical software module, for instance, a developer might initially choose a naive implementation to establish the overall functionality. Once the higher-level abstraction is in place and its dependencies exposed, the developer may identify more efficient algorithms or data structures that could only have become apparent by observing this higher-level vantage point.

In deep learning, higher-level reversal manifests itself in a different manner. Rather than merely focusing on abstraction to manage complexity, deep learning models also incorporate the power of abstraction to uncover and generalize high-level patterns in vast amounts of data. By leveraging many layers of non-linear transformations, artificial neural networks directly learn abstract representations of their input data and make predictions or classifications based on these abstractions.

In deep learning, higher-level reversal typically occurs when a neural network learns to recognize critical patterns by analyzing the intermediate representations of the input in its hidden layers. For instance, in image classification tasks, the lower layers of a convolutional neural network are often responsible for detecting low-level features, such as edges and corners, while the subsequent layers progressively learn higher-level features like shapes, textures, and object parts. This advanced capability is akin to higher-level reversal in computer science, as it involves an iterative process of discovering progressively more abstract representations.

Upon closer examination, we see that while both computer science and deep learning utilize abstraction and higher-level reversal to great effect, the approach and ultimate goals of these distinct fields differ. In computer science, abstraction is employed primarily for simplification and management purposes, whereas in deep learning, abstraction forms the very basis for learning complex patterns and making predictions.

Moreover, the paradigm of abstraction in computer science is fundamentally a human-guided endeavor. Developers and architects decide the right levels of abstraction and design systems accordingly. Contrarily, in deep learning systems, abstraction is self-driven; the neural network uses techniques such as gradient descent and backpropagation to refine its internal representation without human intervention.

As we progress further in our exploration of abstraction, let this contrast serve as a stark reminder of the diverse realms in which abstraction operates, and yet how intertwined its principles are with our pursuits of understanding, organizing, and taming the ever-growing complexity we encounter daily in our world. This fascinating interplay between computer science and deep learning will continue to unravel as we peel back the layers of abstraction, delving into more complex concepts and comparing their applications across various domains. May this journey instill within us a newfound appreciation for the intricate beauty of abstraction and higher-level reversal, and enrich our understanding of the myriad ways in which they shape our problem-solving abilities.

## Examining Attraction to Definitions: How Use Cases Influence Our Choices

Consider the following scenario: a team of engineers is tasked with designing an innovative new software product, one that effectively learns from user

behavior and adapts its functionality accordingly. From the outset, the team
is drawn to a set of existing definitions and categories rooted in established
machine learning techniques. They quickly begin partitioning the problem
space according to these familiar terms - supervised and unsupervised
learning, reinforcement learning, neural networks - and frame their product
design within these well-defined boundaries.

While these categorical definitions provide the team with a scaffolding
upon which to build their ideas, they also exert a subtle influence on their
decision-making and constrain the potential scope of their solution. For
instance, by adopting elements of supervised learning that they had become
familiar within a previous project, they might overlook some promising
unsupervised learning techniques that were more relevant to the problem at
hand. In this way, their attraction to predefined categories exerts both an
enabling and limiting effect on their problem-solving process.

The same dynamic can be seen when we consider another fundamental
component of abstraction: granularity. By shifting our focus from coarse
-grained to fine-grained abstractions, we can achieve a higher degree of
accurateness and precision. But once again, our attachment to definitions
might lead us astray by biasing our initial choice of granularity levels. If
a particular use case has been traditionally dealt with on a higher level of
abstraction, we might be predisposed to continue working on this level, even
if a more fine-grained approach would yield better results.

What, then, can be done to counterbalance this attraction to definitions
and ensure our abstraction strategies remain flexible and context-dependent?
The answer lies in cultivating an acute awareness of our own cognitive
tendencies and developing a critical mindset that questions our default
assumptions.

The first step in this process is acknowledging the powerful role that
definitions play in guiding our choices. It may be helpful to review past
abstraction efforts and identify instances where definitions swayed our
decision-making - for better or for worse. By reflecting on these experiences,
we can begin to develop a more conscious and deliberate approach to
incorporating definitions into our abstraction strategies.

As we become more attuned to the ways in which definitions shape our
thinking, we can also learn to resist their allure by deliberately considering
alternative perspectives. Instead of allowing predefined categories to steer

us towards a particular solution, we can challenge ourselves to explore a wide range of possible use cases, even those that seem to defy established definitions. This willingness to think outside the box might just open up new lines of inquiry and novel solutions that would have remained inaccessible otherwise.

Moreover, it is essential to strike a balance between the desire for precision and the need for adaptability. Definitions should be treated as helpful tools for organizing our thoughts but should not be so rigid as to inhibit creativity and context-dependent problem solving. By seeking a balance between precision and generalization, we can better hone our abstraction skills and ensure that our strategies are optimally tailored to address the complexity and nuance of real-world problems.

In conclusion, our innate attraction to definitions can both empower and hamper our abstraction efforts. However, by cultivating an awareness of this phenomenon and deliberately developing a critical, context-driven approach to abstraction, we can harness the power of definitions while avoiding their potential pitfalls. By embracing a more nuanced, thoughtful, and flexible strategy, we can enhance our capacity for analyzing complex problems and uncovering innovative solutions that might have previously eluded us. Reaping the rewards of such an approach will undoubtedly expand our mindsets and elevate our abstraction expertise, effectively preparing us for the complex challenges that lie ahead.

## The Importance of Nuanced Thinking in Abstraction

Abstraction, at its core, is a powerful cognitive tool that enables humans to navigate complex problems by focusing on what is most pertinent to the task at hand. By filtering out unnecessary details and reducing reality to distilled forms, abstraction provides a scaffold for constructing solutions across various domains of knowledge. However, an underexplored aspect in the discourse on abstraction is the importance of nuanced thinking- that art of skimming the surface and delving beneath the superficial layers when it is warranted. Nuanced thinking enriches the abstraction process, making it more discerning and contextually relevant.

Take, for example, the development of a machine learning algorithm for the early detection of emotion dysregulation - a feature of borderline personality disorders. This algorithm is expected to analyze communication patterns on social media platforms. A purely abstract perspective may reduce this issue to a text classification problem, where the written text is screened for specific keywords or phrases that signify emotion dysregulation. Exporting data, engineering features, and applying statistical models are all essential components. However, nuanced thinking prompts a deeper examination of factors such as users' cultural background, gender, age, and linguistic patterns, all of which influence how emotions manifest on social media outlets.

Moreover, certain manifestations of emotion dysregulation might not be tied to keywords but rather the frequency and manner in which specific phrases and words are employed. Ignoring such subtly embedded cues would lead to oversimplification and miss critical information for accurate prediction. By adopting a nuanced abstraction approach, a more inclusive and context- aware algorithm could better account for the complex interplay of factors that contribute to emotion dysregulation on social media platforms.

Another example comes from the world of business strategy, specifically in the area of market segmentation. A company may identify three primary customer segments based on demographics - millennials, Generation X, and baby boomers. The abstraction process helps the company focus marketing efforts on each segment's specific preferences and needs. However, nuanced thinking uncovers that each generational category comprises various subgroups with distinct preferences, as per their ethnicity, financial habits, personal values, and geographical locations. Thus, by digging deeper and unraveling these subcategories, marketers can devise more tailored and effective strategies for better results.

Nuanced thinking also buffers against overgeneralization and hasty decisions when employing abstraction. Consider a venture capitalist assessing potential investments in the cryptocurrency domain. A purely abstract approach might categorize cryptocurrencies based on market capitalization rankings and utility, such as currency, platform, or utility tokens. The venture capitalist may then allocate resources according to these stripped- down classifications. However, a nuanced approach embraces the messiness and intricacies that underpin the cryptocurrency landscape. It acknowledges factors such as regulatory scrutiny, developer community dynamics, and real- world adoption potential. This more discerning abstraction perspective paves the way for informed decisions and a more resilient investment strategy.

In essence, incorporating nuanced thinking into abstraction is analogous to a skilled painter's attention to detail. While an artist may be adept at creating abstract masterpieces through bold strokes and color blocks, they also understand when to apply subtle shading and fine brushwork to capture the essence of their subject. As practitioners of abstraction, we too must learn to navigate the delicate balance between aggregation and granularity in service of our problem-solving goals.

Taking a cue from the masters of abstraction-be they artists, scientists, or strategists-we too must become adept at recognizing when a touch of nuance could pave the way for breakthrough insights. By embracing the interplay between abstraction and nuanced thinking, we empower ourselves to tackle the multifaceted and multi-layered challenges that define our complex world. As we progress through the evolving landscape of abstraction techniques, the importance of nuance will undoubtedly emerge as a crucial determinant of success for those who truly master the art of abstract thinking.

## Identifying Common Pitfalls and How to Counter Them

In the thrilling journey of harnessing the power of abstraction, we often stumble upon unexpected pitfalls, traps that can easily derail our progress and hamper our ability to think in more nuanced and high-level terms. Identifying these common mistakes and understanding how to counteract them is a crucial element of mastering the art of abstraction. By examining a range of cases across various fields and scenarios, we shall uncover the subtle complexities of navigating the pitfalls and develop strategies to triumph over them.

Consider the early stages of designing a software system: here, functional and modular abstraction practices come into play. Often, inexperienced project teams may fall into the trap of oversimplifying the system by aggressively abstracting its components, causing a loss of vital details needed to address real-world problems. This ambitious drive to simplify can not only lead to wasted resources but also a weaker end product. To counter this, it is crucial to meticulously scrutinize abstract implementations, ensuring they align with the users' needs and provide tangible value.

Another pitfall lies in the domain of physical and temporal abstraction, where abstracting real - world entities and time factors requires careful navigation. Suppose an engineer developing autonomous vehicles excessively abstracts the complexity of a vehicle's engine, discarding details surrounding intricate component interactions and systems management. In this case, the end result will likely fail to account for critical operational nuances and deliver suboptimal performance. To avoid this mistake, engineers ought to strike a balance between abstracting complexity and retaining essential details to accurately represent a system's behavior and interactions.

Recursive abstraction presents its own perils as well. The allure of recursive patterns might entice developers to embed them into a software system without considering possible inefficiencies. Unwarranted or poorly designed recursion can introduce unnecessary complexity and computational burden, resulting in degraded system performance. To evade this, it is essential for developers to rigorously evaluate the appropriateness of recursion in a given situation, ensuring that its benefits outweigh the costs.

As we venture into domains that involve deep learning and artificial intelligence, the significance of questioning assumptions and avoiding false dichotomies reveals itself. Here, the pitfall lies in succumbing to dichotomous viewpoints, driven by simplistic abstractions. For instance, adopting a binary perspective such as "neural networks are either transparent and easy to understand or completely opaque and inscrutable," can obstruct progress in developing new techniques to understand and interpret these complex algorithms. By actively challenging assumptions and systematically breaking away from false dichotomies, we can foster a more nuanced understanding of complex topics and pave the way for innovative approaches to seemingly insurmountable challenges.

Ethical dilemmas, too, lurk in the shadows of abstraction - related endeavors. For example, in the quest to create more efficient algorithms and systems, biased information or representations could harm underrepresented communities, perpetuating inequitable processes and outcomes. Engineers and developers must be careful to recognize unconscious preferences, misrepresentations, and unaddressed biases in their work and deliberately cultivate ethical and inclusive abstraction skills to avoid perpetuating harm.

Countering these pitfalls demands a continuous commitment to introspection, learning, and adaptation. Aspiring abstraction masters must develop habits of self-reflection, evaluating their abstract thinking against real-world expectations and multidimensional criteria to optimize their decision-making and problem-solving abilities. By acknowledging the inherent risks and challenges of abstraction, we can seek to further our understanding and mastery, driving ourselves to conquer the complexities of a rapidly evolving world.

As we tread deeper into the realms of abstraction, we are confronted with a fierce paradox: on one hand, elegance lies in simplicity, but on the other, abstraction is not about reducing complexity but rather navigating it. As we embrace increasing levels of abstraction, we must remain vigilant about the entrapments that lie at every bend. With determination, passion, and strategy, we shall triumphantly steer away from the pitfalls and unleash the power of nuanced thinking to conquer the boundless lands of abstraction.

## Techniques for Improving Context-Awareness and Avoiding Overgeneralization

First and foremost, we must learn to recognize our own cognitive biases, which can distort our perception of the context surrounding a given problem. These biases can include confirmation bias, whereby we selectively notice information that confirms our preconceptions; anchoring bias, by which we give undue influence to the first piece of information we encounter; and availability bias, which leads us to overestimate the importance of particularly salient or memorable examples. By becoming aware of these cognitive biases and deliberately seeking out diverse perspectives and contradictory evidence, we can develop a more well-rounded understanding of the context in which our abstractions are taking place.

Another useful strategy for cultivating context-awareness is to zoom in and out of one's focus, deliberately varying the level of granularity at which one examines a given problem. By zooming in, we can explore the nitty-gritty details of a specific subproblem, which may reveal important contextual cues that might otherwise go unnoticed. Conversely, zooming out allows us to adopt a more holistic perspective, examining the broader environment and identifying overarching patterns that can help to situate our abstraction efforts. Moving between these different levels of focus enables us to strike a balance between simplification and nuance, thus mitigating the risks of overgeneralization.

When it comes to abstraction, questioning one's assumptions is also crucial for fostering context - awareness. By challenging our own assumptions, we may uncover alternative viewpoints or explanations that merit consideration. One way to achieve this is through the use of counterfactuals or thought experiments, which involve imagining alternative scenarios or outcomes in order to explore the robustness of our conclusions. This exercise can help us identify the boundaries of our abstractions and refine our understanding of context.

A convenient way to avoid overgeneralization is to employ multiple models or analogies when abstracting. No single model or analogy can perfectly capture all the complexities of a particular phenomenon. By considering multiple models, we can compensate for the limitations of each individual model and gain a more comprehensive understanding of the situation. This approach is exemplified in the wisdom of the classic saying, "all models are wrong, but some are useful." By juxtaposing different models and analogies, we can triangulate a more accurate picture of reality and avoid the pitfalls of overgeneralizing from one model alone.

Taking into account historical and cross - cultural perspectives is another helpful means of enhancing context - awareness. By examining how similar problems or systems have manifested in different times and cultures, we can gain an appreciation for the diverse factors that shape our experiences and determine which aspects of our current context are truly unique or representative of wider trends. Such analysis can illuminate the deeper forces at work, allowing us to calibrate our abstractions more precisely and avoid overgeneralization.

Finally, embracing humility in the face of complexity is critical for fostering context - awareness and avoiding overgeneralization. This entails acknowledging the limits of our own knowledge and adopting an attitude of curiosity and openness to new information. By recognizing that our abstractions are, by nature, imperfect approximations of reality, we are more likely to maintain an ongoing critical dialogue with our own thinking, refining and revising our abstractions as new information becomes available.

## Case Study: Context - Dependence and Higher - Level Reversal in Product Development

As the sun set over the bustling metropolis of Futura City, a team of product developers gathered in a conference room, embarking on the next phase of their ambitious project. Tasked with designing a state - of - the - art electric scooter, they aimed to revolutionize urban transportation with unparalleled ease of use and exceptional performance. This endeavor would require them to push the limits of abstraction and appreciate the nuances that determine success in the world of product development. Little did they know that context - dependence and higher - level reversal would be integral in navigating the unfolding challenges.

The team, affectionately known as the "Scooter Squad," began by exploring the realm of functional abstraction in their design process. They sought out essential similarities in existing electric scooters and distilled them into core components and processes. While this initial effort helped them filter out less critical features, the team soon encountered a context - dependent issue. They discovered that while most electric scooters were designed for relatively flat terrain, Futura City was distinguished by its hilly landscape. In this unique urban setting, riders required improved battery life and uphill performance, forcing the team to reconsider their initial abstracted design.

As they worked to incorporate the unique characteristics of their target environment, the Scooter Squad was introduced to the concept of higher - level reversal, an idea that deviated from the typical abstraction process. Rather than simplifying complex elements into more general components, higher - level reversal challenged the team to consider additional intricacies that would enhance their product's performance in the demanding context of Futura City.

For example, in response to the hilly terrain, the team explored how regenerative braking, a technology typically reserved for high - end electric vehicles, could be integrated into their scooter design to increase battery life and improve the riding experience. As they delved deeper into this concept, the Scooter Squad discovered that additional complexities, such as increased system weight and a more intricate braking mechanism, had the potential to impact overall performance and usability.

These context - dependent insights guided the team to revise their initial abstraction and gave them a more profound appreciation for the importance of addressing nuances. As a result, they managed to strike a balance between simplifying the scooter's design while refining its capabilities to meet the unique demands of Futura City, thus establishing success in the marketplace.

In working diligently and persistently to manage the dual forces of context-dependence and higher-level reversal, the Scooter Squad develops an electric scooter that not only simplifies the urban commute but thrifes within the challenging parameters of their city streets. They demonstrated the power of adaptability and the benefits of seeking out nontraditional approaches when abstraction appears to lead down a limited path.

As the team celebrated the completion of their design and prepared for production, they took a moment to reflect on the lessons they had learned. They recognized the necessity of embracing complexity, nuance, and context when engaging in abstraction, along with the importance of questioning assumptions and avoiding false dichotomies that can undermine success in product development.

Just as the vibrant city lights illuminating the evening sky of Futura City are inextricably connected to the urban landscape which they define, so too are the intricate relationships between context and abstraction woven into the very fabric of successful product design. By acknowledging and cherishing these subtle interconnections, the Scooter Squad transcended the limitations of traditional abstract thinking and, in doing so, created a product that truly glided through the hills and valleys of the city that inspired it. As the sun rises and sets over Futura City, it casts light upon the future possibilities of abstraction - a world of ever - changing context, complexity, and nuance that invites us all to explore, question, and adapt in our quest for continuous growth and innovation.

## Balancing Precision and Generalization: Focusing on the Right Level of Abstraction

In abstraction, one of the most crucial yet challenging tasks is to strike the perfect balance between precision and generalization. Dance on the razor's edge, and one can crystalize complex information into a profoundly simple, insightful form. Fall, and one risks either sacrificing essential detail or painting with too broad a stroke, rendering abstractions devoid of utility.

To navigate this fine line, we must develop a keen awareness of our context and a discerning capacity to judge the appropriate level of abstraction for the task at hand.

Let us dive into the world of cartography, which offers a compelling analogy for the challenge and necessity of striking this delicate balance. Consider the art of mapmaking, where one must skillfully balance the level of detail with the intended purpose of the map. In essence, mapmakers practice a form of spatial abstraction as they simplify complex terrain, removing extraneous features while retaining those crucial for a map's intended purpose.

Imagine, for example, a hiker planning a trek through a mountain range. She would greatly benefit from a topographical map that highlights the peaks, valleys, and contours of the landscape, allowing her to identify the most suitable route for her journey. Such a map employs a level of abstraction that retains vital details such as elevation, trails, and water sources. Conversely, an airline pilot preparing for a transcontinental flight would derive little value from a topographical map. In this context, the appropriate abstraction might discard most of the map's topography to focus instead on flight routes, waypoints, and airspace boundaries.

This cartography analogy illustrates the importance of understanding the context of a problem and distilling its essence while identifying the right level of abstraction. Applying this discernment in a practical scenario, let us consider the abstraction process in software development, combed from the experiences of a seasoned developer. When designing the architecture for a new application, the developer must balance the desire to avoid premature optimization - generalizing too broadly - with the need to include sufficient detail and specificity to ensure efficient and scalable execution - abstraction with precision.

For instance, she embarked on a project to modernize a legacy e - commerce platform. Initially, her team proposed a new design that featured highly generic components that could handle various types of transactions and customer interactions seamlessly. The enticement of a scalable, all - encompassing application seemed like the apt solution, given the position of the rapidly growing e - commerce market.

However, something seemed amiss. The team noticed that the high degree of generalization obscured essential details crucial for efficient implementation. By overgeneralizing the platform and trying to cater to every possible scenario, the development process became bloated, and the product felt unwieldy and difficult to understand.

Drawing on her expertise in abstraction, the developer prompted her team to revisit the system's requirements and goals. An in-depth analysis revealed that despite the potential for various transaction types, the current needs of the business only necessitated a small subset of these capabilities. With this newfound insight, the team pivoted their approach and identified an appropriate level of abstraction, gleaning the system's essential details while retaining necessary flexibility for the future.

With this refined architecture, her team capitalized on a precise abstraction that conserved crucial elements for an efficient and comprehensive platform. The project thrived, and the balanced approach proved essential in successfully executing the modernization effort.

In conclusion, the challenge of abstraction lies not only in discerning the boundaries that separate vital details from superfluity but also in determining the optimal level of abstraction for a particular context. The elusive equilibrium may appear as a mirage at first; however, honing one's understanding of context-dependence and maintaining a keen eye on the crux of the problem we face brings the power of artful abstraction into grasp. As we continue probing abstraction techniques, let us keep in mind the delicate dance between precision and generalization, embracing the nuance that lies at the heart of mastering this powerful cognitive tool.

## Reflection and Continuous Improvement: Cultivating Your Art of Nuance Skills

The art of nuance is a refined skill that involves the delicate balancing act of navigating the complex world of abstraction. It is a journey filled with exploration, introspection, and constant iteration, much like the artistic process itself. As practitioners and learners of abstraction, we must continue to refine our craft, adapting our skills and knowledge to better seep into the intricacies of an ever-changing landscape. It is through this dedication to reflection and continuous improvement that we cultivate our art of nuance skills and fully harness the benefits of abstraction.

Let us examine a real-world example of reflection and continuous im-

provement in the realm of software engineering. Imagine a team responsible
for designing and maintaining a highly complex and modular software system. Over time, the team members refine the system's components, adding
layers of abstraction and decoupling the modules, striving for increased
flexibility and simplicity. Yet, in an annual review, they find that the system
remains difficult to navigate and modify despite their efforts. Instead of
solely attributing this issue to technical debt or complexity, the members
decide to take a step back, reflecting on their understanding and application of abstraction principles. They engage in retrospectives, study group
discussions, and individual self-critiques to identify areas of improvement
and question their assumptions.

Through these activities, the team realizes that their abstraction process
overlooked certain nuances in the system's domain. In some cases, they had
overgeneralized, creating abstractions that hid essential details and hampered
adaptability. In other instances, they discovered that false dichotomies had
led to convoluted dependencies between components, undermining their
efforts at decoupling.

With newfound insights, the team embarks on an iterative journey to
refine their abstraction strategies. They opt for smaller and more focused
retrospectives after each release, encouraging an ongoing dialogue and
reflection on their understanding of abstraction principles. By fostering a
culture of continuous learning, the team members attend workshops, explore
new domains, and mentor each other to expand their collective knowledge
of abstraction techniques.

One year later, the team holds another annual review. Their system
exhibits greater clarity and flexibility, thanks to their dedication to the art
of nuance and reflection. They have successfully adopted a more mindful
approach to abstraction and better appreciate the importance of examining
the context deeply before applying such techniques.

The software engineering team's experience mirrors the broader journey
we must all embark on when striving to cultivate our art of nuance skills.
As learners of abstraction, we must commit to reflection and continuous
improvement in much the same way an artist continually refines their
technique. This may involve engaging in critical thinking exercises to
question our assumptions and beliefs about abstraction or exploring new
domains and perspectives to widen our knowledge.

Measuring progress in our journey to master abstraction may not be as explicit as ticking off a list of milestones. However, it is through the incremental improvements in our approach and thought process that our growth becomes evident. Whether it is the ability to identify common pitfalls and avoid them proactively or the refinement of our intuition about what constitutes the appropriate level of abstraction, these achievements reflect our progress in mastering the art of nuance.

As we look back on our journey and the path that lies ahead, we must remember that the pursuit of nuance in abstraction is a lifelong endeavor, a continuous dance between simplification and the retention of essential details. Through each encounter with abstraction, we grow and enrich our understanding, adding color and depth to our mental palette. Ultimately, it is this commitment to reflection and continuous improvement that will empower us to become master artists in navigating and managing complexity in an ever-changing world. So, let the music of abstraction continue to play, and let us dance its rhythm with the elegance and grace of a true master of the art of nuance.

# Chapter 5

# Questioning Assumptions, Avoiding False Dichotomies, and Purposeful Abstraction Tailoring

Questioning assumptions, avoiding false dichotomies, and purposeful abstraction tailoring are critical facets in the abstract thinker's toolkit, clearing the path to meaningful simplification of the complex world. At its core, abstraction is meant to facilitate problem-solving and enable a clearer understanding of the subject matter; however, when assumptions go unchallenged, false dichotomies take root, and abstractions are not tailored appropriately, the very purpose of abstraction is undermined.

Let us consider the scenario of a software development team trying to design the architecture of a new application. The team applies functional and modular abstraction to break down the application into smaller, manageable units. Through each level of abstraction, members of the team make a series of implicit assumptions about the functionality, scope, and feasibility of the project. However, failing to question these assumptions can lead to blind spots in the abstraction process, which may manifest as bugs or design flaws when the system is implemented.

For instance, the team might assume that data storage and retrieval requirements will remain constant over time, relying on a traditional relational database management system. If this assumption goes unchallenged and actual usage patterns reveal a significant increase in data storage and retrieval needs, the application's performance could suffer, and potentially degrade the entire system. By questioning these assumptions early in the abstraction process, the team may have chosen a more scalable solution, such as a NoSQL database or distributed cloud storage.

False dichotomies further complicate the abstraction process. In the same software development scenario, suppose the team is faced with the decision between adopting an Agile or Waterfall software development process. The Agile approach emphasizes flexibility and rapid iteration, while Waterfall follows a fixed plan. The team may feel constrained to choose between these two approaches, each with its pros and cons. This false dichotomy obscures other alternatives that could be more suitable for the project. A more effective approach might involve blending the two methodologies, perhaps utilizing Agile for front - end development and Waterfall for foundational back - end components.

Purposeful abstraction tailoring is a crucial skill that involves determining the appropriate level of abstraction to suit one's context. An overly simplistic abstraction may leave out essential details, while an excessively complex abstraction can obfuscate crucial information. In our software development scenario, consider the task of developing a machine learning model to predict user behavior in the application. Too much abstraction may ignore important nuances in the data and lead to poor predictive performance, while too little abstraction can result in excessive computational demand and an unwieldy model.

Mastery of these three aspects-questioning assumptions, avoiding false dichotomies, and purposeful abstraction tailoring-empowers abstract thinkers to navigate the delicate balance between simplicity and complexity. Through continual practice and reflection, one can refine their skills and achieve greater precision in understanding and solving intricate problems.

As we progress beyond this topic, we delve into the art of retaining critical information while abstracting, addressing another vital aspect of successful abstraction: the interplay between simplification and maintaining essential details. This investigation will enhance our perspectives on abstraction techniques and add depth to our understanding of the intricate process that governs discerning the signal from the noise in our complex world.

## Introduction to Questioning Assumptions, Avoiding False Dichotomies, and Purposeful Abstraction Tailoring

To begin with, it is vital to question the assumptions that underpin our abstractions. Every abstraction is, to some extent, an approximation of reality, and our beliefs about the essential elements of a problem or system are often influenced by personal experiences, biases, or prevailing cultural norms. Consider, for example, the computer scientist - turned - startup - founder who, drawing from her background in algorithmic optimization, seeks to streamline her company's human resources division through a rigid, rules - based approach.

Though the founder's experience in computer science may yield valuable insights, it is crucial to recognize the inherent limitations of viewing a complex, human - centered system through such a narrow, computation - oriented lens. By questioning assumptions and considering alternative perspectives, the founder may more effectively uncover the true needs, motives, and dynamics at play in her organization and devise more contextually appropriate strategies for improvement.

Likewise, avoiding false dichotomies is crucial to responsible abstraction. False dichotomies, also known as false binaries, arise when we oversimplify reality by boiling complex phenomena down to two opposing categories. For instance, consider the classic false dichotomy of "nature versus nurture" - the long - standing debate over whether an individual's characteristics are primarily determined by genetics or their environment. This simplistic abstraction glosses over the countless intricacies and interactions at play in human development and perpetuates deep - seated misunderstandings about human potential and identity.

To avoid falling into this all - too - common trap, it is essential to recognize and challenge the false dichotomies embedded in our abstractions. To do so, one could use the lenses of nuance and empathy, broadening our understanding of the problem space and embracing the messiness and complexity of the real world.

Finally, purposeful abstraction tailoring involves adapting abstractions to the unique context and constraints of the problem at hand. Rather than indiscriminately applying our favorite or most familiar tools - be they frameworks, theories, or mental models - we must deliberately select and adjust our abstractions to fit the contours of the problem at hand.

Consider a seasoned software architect tasked with designing a system for predicting crop yields based on remote sensing data. While the architect may be skilled in creating elegant, scalable solutions for large - scale data processing, this task requires more than just optimizing code. To succeed, she must not only study the intricacies of the agricultural domain - from climatic patterns to soil chemistry - but also tailor her abstractions to account for these domain - specific factors.

In other words, when navigating the complex and ever - changing landscape of real - world problems, it is crucial to remember that not all abstractions are created equal. By critically examining our assumptions, avoiding false dichotomies, and purposefully tailoring our abstractions to fit the problem at hand, we can more effectively harness the power of abstraction and unlock new pathways to growth and understanding.

## The Importance of Challenging Assumptions in Abstraction: Tools and Techniques for Examining Beliefs

The art of abstraction is a cognitive dance as old as human ingenuity itself. To bend and mold our comprehension of the world around us, we rely on this innate capacity to synthesize complex systems into simplified representations. In doing so, we are - consciously and unconsciously - making assumptions about the subject at hand. In some situations, assumptions serve as useful heuristics that enable efficient decision - making. However, assumptions can also stifle creative solutions and blind us to novel insights. Thus, learning to challenge our assumptions is a crucial aspect of mastering the art of abstraction.

Abstraction allows us to navigate the intricate web of reality by drawing essential details and discarding irrelevant information. Consistently asking "Why?" peels back the layers of our beliefs, compelling us to dissect the very foundations of our assumptions.

Let us explore the importance of challenging assumptions in abstraction through the story of Alex, a gifted engineer tasked with designing a new suspension system for an off - road vehicle. Alex, aware of their role in the development of a cutting-edge product, embarks on their research with vigor, immersing themselves in the world of suspension systems. Much to their astonishment, Alex uncovers a myriad of traditional assumptions that have guided the designs within this niche for decades.

Instead of accepting these assumptions as immutable truths, Alex engages in a process of radical doubt, critically examining each belief they encounter. "Why must a suspension system react to the ground?" they muse, questioning the fundamental premise upon which all suspension systems thus far have been built.

Through this process of intellectual skepticism, Alex stumbles upon an unexpected revelation: perhaps the modern ideal of a reactive suspension system is unhelpful, or even counterproductive, for an off-road vehicle. This insight leads Alex to a groundbreaking idea: a proactive suspension system that anticipates the terrain ahead, rather than simply reacting to it.

Alex's story illustrates the transformative power of challenging assumptions in abstraction. By questioning the conventional wisdom within their field, Alex birthed an innovative solution that challenged the status quo. Their willingness to wrestle with established beliefs allowed for a rich exploration of more nuanced, context-dependent nuances in suspension system development.

To replicate Alex's achievements and sharpen our abilities to challenge our assumptions, we must expand our analytic toolkit. One such tool is the Socratic method, which emphasizes critical thinking through dialogue and inquiry. By encouraging others to challenge our beliefs and assumptions, we can expose gaps in our understanding and reevaluate the scope of our abstractions.

Another useful technique to examine assumptions is counterfactual reasoning, where hypothetical scenarios are analyzed and evaluated. Exploring "what-if" scenarios exposes the fragility of our assumptions, and, ultimately, their influence over our abstraction processes.

Consider a policy maker responsible for drafting an emergency-response plan for a city coping with a pandemic. Before crafting the details, they must first question the assumptions that underscore their policy framework. Are they assuming that the healthcare system will remain resilient? Or that citizens will comply with emergency mandates? By challenging these assumptions and undertaking counterfactual reasoning, the policy maker can devise a more comprehensive and robust response plan that accounts for a broader range of potential scenarios.

As Picasso, the great virtuoso of abstract art, once said, "Art is the lie that enables us to realize the truth." In the same vein, abstraction allows us to navigate the labyrinthine world by distilling complexity into simplified models. However, we must remain ever-vigilant in the pursuit of questioning our assumptions. As we strive to hone our abstractive capabilities, let us not shy away from the discomfort of challenging deeply-held beliefs.

By embracing uncertainty, we forge a richer, more discerning intellect and ensure that our abstractions remain truthful navigators in the journey of understanding. As we progress from the realm of examining assumptions into the treacherous landscape of false dichotomies, we are well-equipped to dissect the oversimplifications that may taint our abstract reasoning abilities. So, ready yourself for a rigorous exercise of mental agility, for it is by defying the status quo that we elevate our abstract thinking to new heights.

## Recognizing and Breaking Apart False Dichotomies: The Harmful Consequences of Oversimplified Abstraction

In the realm of abstraction, perhaps the most insidious obstacle to achieving a deep understanding of a subject is the false dichotomy: the notion that there exist only two mutually exclusive options, when in fact the matter at hand harbors countless shades of gray. Such oversimplification can impede problem-solving, stunt creativity, and ossify ingrained prejudices, all while masquerading under the guise of simplicity or elegance. To engage in truly effective and nuanced abstract thinking, we must be able to identify these false dichotomies and move beyond their binary limitations.

Before launching into examples and technical insights, it's crucial to establish some basic mechanisms for recognizing false dichotomies. To detect whether a given scenario has been oversimplified, consider these three hallmarks of a false dichotomy:

1. The scenario demands an either/or choice between two options; 2. The premises on which these options are based are mutually exclusive but not jointly exhaustive; 3. Upon closer inspection, one can identify further alternatives or synthesizing options that defy the binary choice.

Let us now venture into concrete examples, illustrating how these pernicious foes of clear thinking have managed to infiltrate various fields.

Consider the computer science conundrum of whether to prioritize speed
or space in an algorithm's design. At its core, this is a false dichotomy:
skilled engineers can devise techniques that allow for high efficiency in terms
of both time and memory. For instance, they might exploit the principle of
'caching' to minimize time spent retrieving data or apply the B-tree data
structure to ensure both excellent search performance and optimal use of
memory. Thus, rather than confining themselves to only one of two options,
computer scientists break the illusory constraints of a false dichotomy and
produce creative solutions in the process.

False dichotomies may also rear their heads within the world of strategic
planning. Perhaps none is more pernicious than the age-old debate between
centralized and decentralized decision-making. Throughout history, the
pendulum of thought would periodically swing between these two options,
but the false dichotomy here is that organizations might simply be better off
with a mix of centralization and decentralization, harnessing the strengths
of both approaches. By acknowledging this third option, the savvy strategist
can craft a more flexible and adaptive organization suited for the complexities
of the modern world.

Recognizing false dichotomies is only half the battle; we must dispense
with their harmful consequences as well. By indulging in oversimplified and
binary thinking, we can fall prey to a host of negative outcomes:

1. Prematurely discarding potential solutions: By narrowing our focus
to two options, we may be blind to alternative or hybrid solutions that lie
outside the imposed confines.

2. Stymieing creativity: False dichotomies can limit our ability to think
innovatively and outside the box, as we may feel forced to work within
predetermined, binary parameters.

3. Reinforcing cognitive biases: False dichotomies can serve as self-
fulfilling prophecies, allowing preexisting beliefs and prejudices to go unchallenged by alternative perspectives.

In order to break apart false dichotomies and liberate our abstract
thinking from their grip, we should strive to undertake the following steps:

1. Challenge assumptions: Unmask the hidden premises that underlie
the presented options and consider whether they are truly immutable.

2. Apply the principle of synthesis: Seek unifying or reconciling solutions that incorporate the strengths of both options while mitigating their weaknesses.

3. Engage in divergent thinking: Encourage exploration of alternative possibilities, even if they initially seem counterintuitive or far-flung.

The abstract thinker's crusade against false dichotomies is one that will span the entirety of their intellectual journey. As we arm ourselves with awareness, analysis, and synthesis, becoming ever more vigilant against the pitfalls of oversimplification, we may find that previously undiscovered and promising paths arise from the vapor of false dichotomies. The ultimate reward, then, is the privilege of navigating these novel pathways, uncovering diverse and surprising insights along the way - and realizing that the riches of understanding reside not in simple binaries but in the multifaceted tapestry of possibilities that lie just beyond their reach.

## Purposeful Abstraction Tailoring: Identifying the Appropriate Level of Abstraction for Your Context

The old maxim, "less is more," can often ring true when it comes to abstraction. Simplifying complex problems into their essential elements allows us to process and understand them more easily. However, our pursuit of simplicity should be tempered with the recognition that sometimes, more is more, and retaining a certain level of detail is critical to accurately represent the problem at hand. This balance is achieved through purposeful abstraction tailoring, where we strive to find the appropriate level of abstraction for our specific context.

Consider an architect designing a building. If she were to work at too high of a level of abstraction, her designs might consist only of basic geometric shapes with no indication of scale, materials, or functional requirements. In contrast, if the architect produced overly detailed schematics, her colleagues would be overwhelmed with unnecessary information, making it difficult for them to grasp how elements of the design work together. By using the guiding notion of purposeful abstraction tailoring, she can strike the optimal balance between simplification and detail, retaining key elements that allow her design to be practical, comprehensible, and able to be implemented efficiently.

Achieving the optimal level of abstraction takes consideration of the following factors:

1. Audience: Abstractions should be tailored to meet the needs of the specific group assessing or using them. An executive will require a higher level of abstraction to make strategic decisions compared to a software engineer who will need more specific details to build a product. Cater to the recipient's needs while remaining cognizant of the risk of oversimplification.

Take, for example, the case of a software developer presenting the design of a new system to both the engineering team and the management team. By preparing two distinct, tailor-made abstractions, she can present the necessary amount of detail for each group, enhancing overall understanding and efficiency within the organization.

2. Intent: Focusing on the purpose or goal of the abstraction is critical. If the goal is to identify patterns or trends, a higher level of abstraction may be useful. Conversely, if the aim is to troubleshoot a specific issue or test a hypothesis, more detail may be required. Balance the drive for simplicity with the objective of the abstraction.

Imagine a data scientist working on a problem that requires identifying relationships between different variables. By abstracting overly specific details that do not contribute to those relationships, he can concentrate on larger patterns that emerge within the data, enabling him to identify the core variables driving the outcome.

3. Adaptability: Tailoring abstraction to be adaptable across different contexts and scenarios can maximize its utility. Modifying abstraction levels can enable more effective problem solving, communication, and cooperation across diverse groups and situations.

Consider a team of designers working on a product for a global market. By employing a flexible approach to abstraction and incorporating diverse perspectives and contexts, they can create a product that appeals to a wider range of users while avoiding a one-size-fits-all solution that may fall short of satisfying any specific market.

Identifying the appropriate level of abstraction is a balancing act, moderated by several variables: subjectivity, detail, and pattern recognition. Striking the right balance can have a profound impact on the effectiveness of our decision-making processes and the ultimate outcomes of our endeavors. We must resist the temptation of falling into the trap of oversimplification or retreating into the comfort of excessive minutiae.

In conclusion, the art of abstraction is a dynamic and nuanced process that requires a keen mastery of balance, adaptability, and context-awareness. By embracing purposeful abstraction tailoring, we enable ourselves to navigate the complex terrains of our respective fields while maximizing our cognitive and problem-solving capabilities. By refining our skill in this practice, we unlock the ability to access higher-level insights and make strides toward achieving our goals. As we strive for mastery in abstraction, we must remember that the ultimate purpose is not to paint the world in its most minimal or most intricate form, but rather to find the harmony that lies between the two, fostering a rich, multifaceted understanding of the world around us.

## Practical Examples: Questioning Assumptions and Avoiding False Dichotomies in Software Architecture, Product Development, and Strategic Planning

One often encounters a myriad of assumptions and dichotomies in the complex world of software architecture, product development, and strategic planning. These assumptions, although helpful simplifications, can sometimes become limiting factors. As we set out to question such assumptions and to challenge false dichotomies, it is crucial to consider practical examples where this mindset can bring substantial value and improvements.

Let us first explore the realm of software architecture. Consider the ubiquitous client-server model, a fundamental assumption governing the organization and interaction of many software systems. While this model offers significant benefits in terms of manageability and scalability, it might not be the best approach in cases of highly distributed or peer-to-peer systems. By challenging this client-server assumption, architects can broaden their horizons and consider novel solutions, such as the Distributed Hash Table, which underpins BitTorrent, one of the most successful peer-to-peer file-sharing systems.

Moreover, software architects often fall prey to the false dichotomy of monolithic architecture versus microservices. Although monolithic systems have been criticized for lower maintainability, more challenging deployments, and scalability limitations, they can be the ideal choice for smaller, straightforward applications that do not warrant the operational overhead or complexity of microservices. By avoiding the trap of a binary choice between monolithic and microservices architectures, architects can explore hybrid approaches that incorporate elements from both ends of the spectrum, adapting the architecture to best suit system requirements and constraints.

In product development, practitioners frequently encounter the well-known waterfall versus agile dichotomy. While waterfall has its roots in linearity and rigidity, and agile in flexibility and adaptability, blindly treating them as polar opposites can be counterproductive. A study conducted by Karlsson and Åhlström (2004) emphasizes the applicability of a combination of waterfall and agile practices in certain scenarios. For instance, a team might leverage agile concepts in planning and requirement elicitation, aided by frequent communication and feedback, but adopt a more stepwise approach in development, testing, and deployment phases, preserving control and predictability. By questioning the assumption of an either-or choice between agile and waterfall, product development teams can adapt and tailor their processes to better fit the context of the project.

Assumptions related to commoditization and customization are often encountered in strategic planning. At one extreme lie businesses offering commoditized products that emphasize economies of scale and low price; at the other lies the realm of deeply customized offerings that cater to unique customer needs. But decision-makers often fail to realize that sometimes the best approach lies in crafting tailored combinations of standardized and customized offerings. Apple Inc.'s approach is an archetypal example: offering a wide range of devices and products catering to different customer preferences, yet maintaining an air of exclusivity and customization through personalized in-store experiences, product engraving, and augmenting customer service. By avoiding the false dichotomy between commoditization and customization, strategists can develop a business model that blends the best of both worlds, maximizing opportunities for growth.

These practical, real-world examples reveal that questioning assumptions and challenging false dichotomies promotes creativity, flexibility, and adaptability in software architecture, product development, and strategic planning. By leveraging this mindset in our professional undertakings, we can foster a more nuanced understanding of the dynamics at play and deliver better outcomes.

Just as one would think twice about putting on a pair of shoes made for someone else's feet, professionals should pause and think critically about the assumptions we accept without question. Pitfalls of assumptions and false dichotomies lie dormant until we uncover them, armed with a newfound enquiring spirit and readiness to adapt. Having conquered this terrain, we now venture to an even more significant frontier: the role of intuition and cognitive biases in abstraction. By learning to navigate and mitigate these influences, we will arrive even closer to the mastery of our chosen domains.

## The Role of Intuition and Cognitive Biases in Abstraction: How to Navigate and Mitigate Their Effects

As we delve further into the realm of abstraction, understanding the impact of intuition and cognitive biases on our ability to effectively operate at higher levels of thinking becomes essential. Intuition, that innate sense of knowing without recourse to conscious reasoning, often plays a critical role in the abstraction process. However, it is also subject to various cognitive biases - mental shortcuts that shape our perceptions and judgments in potentially misleading ways.

To begin with, let's consider the role of intuition in abstraction. Our intuitive judgments are often fast and effortless, enabling us to swiftly condense complex information and identify patterns that elude slower, more deliberate forms of reasoning. However, this speed and ease come at a cost, as intuition is more prone to error and subject to cognitive biases.

One example of a cognitive bias that affects intuition in abstraction is the availability heuristic. This mental shortcut leads to a tendency to overestimate the importance of readily accessible information simply because it is easy to recall. In the context of abstraction, this might mean that we prematurely dismiss certain details as superfluous, merely because they are not immediately apparent or emotionally salient. Conversely, we might assign too much significance to factors that come readily to mind, even if they are not critical to the problem at hand.

Another cognitive bias that plays a role in abstraction is confirmation bias, the inclination to search for, interpret, and remember information in a way that validates our existing beliefs and expectations. When engaging in abstraction, it can distort our perception of shared structures and lead to an exaggerated emphasis on similarities while downplaying dissimilarities. This may result in an oversimplified abstraction that supports our preconceptions but fails to account for crucial contextual differences.

Anchoring, another cognitive bias, occurs when we rely too heavily on an initial piece of information when making decisions. In abstraction, we might anchor our understanding of a problem or system based on an initial simplification or shared structure, which may not fully capture the essential complexity of the situation. Consequently, this anchoring can lead us to underestimate the impact of additional information or changes in context as we refine our abstraction.

So, how can we navigate and mitigate the effects of intuition and cognitive biases in abstraction? The first step is awareness. Being conscious of the existence of cognitive biases and their potential impact on our thinking enables us to question our assumptions and reevaluate our abstractions when necessary.

Next, we should foster a curious mindset that seeks disconfirming evidence and counterexamples. This approach can counteract the confirmation bias and help us overcome the limitations imposed by our intuitions. By actively searching for information that contradicts our initial beliefs or assumptions, we can refine our abstractions and discover new shared structures that might otherwise have been overlooked.

Another valuable strategy is to embrace collaboration and incorporate diverse perspectives when engaging in abstraction. Actively seeking input from individuals with different backgrounds, expertise, and points of view can help mitigate the influence of cognitive biases and intuitive errors. The collective intelligence of a diverse group can enrich the abstraction process by revealing hidden complexities and questioning assumptive shortcuts.

Finally, to temper the impact of cognitive biases and intuition, we should cultivate the habit of testing and validating our abstractions against real-world data and feedback. This process of iterative refinement encourages continuous improvement and helps ensure that our abstractions remain grounded in reality, avoiding pitfalls associated with oversimplification and overgeneralization.

In closing, intuition and cognitive biases are intertwined elements of our abstract thinking that, if left unchecked, can hinder our capacity to develop nuanced and accurate abstractions. Becoming aware of these influences, questioning our assumptions, embracing collaboration, and iteratively refining our mental models are all crucial steps in navigating the potentially treacherous waters of abstraction. As we endeavor to manage complexity in our increasingly intricate world, developing the art of abstraction while overcoming cognitive biases and intuitive pitfalls will be an essential skill for success.

Such mastery, however, requires investigating common pitfalls and how to counter them. In the next discussion, we will explore techniques for improving context - awareness, avoiding overgeneralization, and ultimately enhancing our abstraction skills.

## Building a Strong Foundation: Clarifying the Purpose and Scope of Your Abstraction Efforts

Purposeful abstraction requires understanding not just the "how" but the "why" of the essential details we extract. Consider, for instance, the world of project management. Project managers routinely break down complex challenges into manageable tasks, often by constructing Gantt charts or other timelines. However, effective time management depends on understanding why certain tasks are important and how they relate to the project's ultimate goals. Identifying a task's purpose is crucial for understanding the relevant details and deciding how much weight to give them in decision-making. This understanding also helps identify and prioritize opportunities for further abstraction.

Let's consider a real - world example: designing a city's public transportation system. Suppose our goal is to reduce traffic congestion, improve air quality, and create a more sustainable urban environment. By explicitly stating these objectives, we provide a clear purpose for the abstraction process. Instead of merely focusing on superficial data like the number of bus routes, number of bus stops, or fleet size, we can start by abstracting higher - order insights: How might different routes intersect to minimize redundancies? What areas of the city need improved service to meet our goals?

Moreover, each of these abstracted insights must be grounded in reality, with due consideration for the constraints imposed by the city's geography, population distribution, zoning requirements, and existing infrastructure.

With the ultimate purpose in mind, we can then ensure that our abstractions are aligned with our broader goals and objectives.

Now that we have a clear purpose in mind, we also need to establish the scope of our abstraction efforts. In other words, how far should our simplifications go? What aspects of reality are critical to retain, and which can be safely discarded? Scoping abstraction is often challenging because it requires striking a delicate balance between simplification and retaining the subtleties that differentiate reality.

To illustrate this point, let us revisit the aforementioned public transportation example. It is necessary to understand the city's current infrastructure, zoning, and population distribution to design an efficient system. Yet, we must also be mindful not to get bogged down in details, such as historical data on past planning decisions or detailed zoning regulations, if they do not contribute meaningfully to our specific goals of reducing traffic congestion and improving air quality.

In scoping abstraction efforts, various questions can help identify the proper balance:

- Which aspects of reality are most closely related to our primary objectives? - How much simplification can be tolerated while maintaining accuracy and efficacy? - Can subproblems be abstracted within their specific domains, or is a more holistic approach necessary? - Are certain details better left to subject matter experts or specialized tools?

Asking these questions throughout the abstraction process enables us to determine which pieces of information are essential, while eliminating the unnecessary clutter that can hamper our overall decision-making ability.

Ultimately, abstraction is an iterative, nuanced process that begins with a strong foundation of purpose and scope. By clearly outlining the objectives and aligning the abstraction process with real-world constraints and complexities, we set the stage for more targeted, efficient strategies in problem-solving and decision-making. Remember, becoming a master of abstraction is akin to a surgeon sharpening their scalpel - with purpose and precision, they can skillfully balance between simplicity and reality, optimizing their methods to deliver exceptional outcomes. As we move on to our next topic, consider how our discussion on purposeful and scoped abstraction sets the stage for exploring context-awareness in abstract thinking, enabling us to counter overgeneralization while retaining the power of abstraction.

## The Iterative Process: Continuously Refining and Adapting Your Abstraction Methods for Optimal Results

In a world where technology is ever-changing and complex problems are on the rise, abstraction is a vital cognitive skill that assists us in simplifying and understanding intricate systems. However, just like any other skill, the art of abstraction requires continuous refinement and adaptation to its methods for achieving optimal results. This iterative process ensures that your abstraction strategies remain relevant, efficient, and effective despite the changing landscapes of various domains.

Consider an expert chef working on their signature dish. Initially, they may experiment with different ingredients and cooking techniques to find the perfect balance of flavors. Over time, new ingredients might be discovered, or perhaps better cooking methods are introduced, prompting the chef to revisit their dish, refine their techniques and adapt to these changes. Just like the chef, practicing the art of abstraction requires a similar dedication to continuous iterations, adjusting our approaches, and learning new techniques as we grow and evolve.

One of the first steps in the iterative process of refining your abstraction methods is assessing the effectiveness of your current strategies. This can be done by evaluating the outcomes of your abstract thinking in tackling problems or exploring complex topics. Did your approach lead to a greater understanding? Did it simplify the problem on hand or allow for more efficient solutions? Reflecting on the successes and failures of past experiences can provide valuable insight, helping you pinpoint strengths or weaknesses in your abstraction strategies.

Having assessed the effectiveness of your current approach, the next step is to explore other strategies that may yield better results. This pursuit involves staying abreast of the latest advancements in fields such as computer science, AI, data science, and other domains, as they offer new techniques and abstraction models that can be utilized across different problem-solving scenarios. Engaging in workshops, seminars, or even online courses can help expand your repertoire of abstraction approaches and ensure that you're well-equipped to tackle any complexity thrown your way.

Experimentation is also a key factor in refining your methods. Various scenarios will require different abstraction techniques, and it's crucial to be open to exploring every option to find what works best for each situation. This may involve switching between modular, functional, or physical abstraction as needed or even combining methods if the situation demands it. Implementing uncommon methods might also yield better outcomes, making it essential to tap into your creativity and challenge the norm.

Collaboration with others plays a significant role in the iterative process of abstraction. Identifying mentors, peers, or colleagues that excel in abstract thinking can expose you to new perspectives and techniques. Engaging in collaborative problem‑solving activities will help broaden your knowledge and your understanding of how others approach abstraction. Regular feedback exchange among your circle can also facilitate improvement in your strategies, as constructive criticism allows for effective adjustments.

Ultimately, continuously refining and adapting your abstraction methods is an ongoing and somewhat recursive process. As your skills and understanding evolve, so too will your ability to recognize what level of abstraction is most effective or when a particular approach is yielding the best results. Patience and persistence are vital, as mastery in the art of abstraction does not come overnight. It requires constant learning, questioning assumptions, and embracing change; all toward achieving those optimal results and deeper understanding of the world we navigate.

As you embark on your journey towards abstraction mastery, remember that change is the only constant, perpetually reshaping the landscapes around us. Embrace this flux, for it is within this ever‑changing terrain that the seeds of ingenuity can find fertile ground and where your abstraction strategies will bloom, leading you to transcend the bounds of conventional thinking, and unlock the true power of the art of abstraction.

## Conclusion: Developing a Mindful Abstraction Practice to Enhance Decision Making and Problem Solving

Throughout this book, we have embarked on a journey to understand the intricate and sophisticated domain of abstraction, delving deep into its various forms, applications, and nuances. A steadfast companion in our quest to manage complexity in a rapidly evolving world, abstraction has repeatedly proven to be a vital cognitive tool for comprehending problems at a higher level. As we approach the culmination of our expedition, it is crucial to reflect on the key insights gained and integrate the knowledge acquired into a mindful abstraction practice to enhance our decision-making and problem-solving capabilities.

An essential part of this practice is developing a balanced and nuanced approach to abstraction. Equipped with this mindset, as one encounters complexity, they can strategically abstract information and reason effectively without being hindered by excessive details or misled by inappropriate simplifications. This attitude is fostered by honing an array of cognitive skills, ranging from challenging assumptions and defying false dichotomies, to retaining essential details and promoting diversity and inclusion in our abstract thinking endeavors.

To construct a foundation for mindful abstraction, our journey has led us through the realms of computer science, deep learning, conceptual reasoning, software architecture, and product development, where we have discovered an array of techniques to recognize and leverage shared structures while discarding superfluous details. These lessons learned are by no means the final destination but rather stepping stones to broader horizons. As with any complex cognitive tool, our ability to wield abstraction adroitly comes primarily through persistent practice, reflection, and adaptation.

A memorable analogy that encapsulates the spirit of mindful abstraction is that of an expert potter at work. Just as the potter takes a lump of clay, carefully removes excess material, and skillfully molds it into the intended shape, we too must extract the essence from complex situations, discard irrelevant information, and sculpt our mental models to accurately represent reality. However, the art of the potter transcends mere technical prowess; a deep understanding of the material, purpose, and context guides their hands to create a harmonious balance between form and function. Similarly, our abstraction practice must be grounded in an unwavering appreciation for the nuances, intricacies, and subtleties of the problems we encounter and the domains in which we apply our skills.

Setting forth with the insights gleaned on this exploration, we must maintain an unwavering commitment to continuous improvement and growth. We should relentlessly question our existing beliefs, remain open to emerging methodologies, and strive to cultivate an insatiable intellectual curiosity.

As we progress, our intuitive grasp of abstraction will deepen, leading to breakthroughs in our problem‑solving and decision‑making prowess. We must, however, always remain cognizant of the potential pitfalls associated with abstraction, exhibiting caution and diligence while navigating the delicate balance between simplification and precision.

Invariably, the domains and challenges we face will continue to evolve for a single immutable truth remains constant: our world will continue to grow in complexity. As the threads of technology and human ingenuity intertwine ever closer, abstraction remains a guiding light illuminating the labyrinthine paths before us. While we cannot predict the precise contour of the journey ahead, armed with the knowledge and skills imparted through this book, we will find ourselves well‑prepared to forge our way forward, charting brave new territories and expanding the frontiers of human understanding.

# Chapter 6

# Frameworks for Practical Application: AI Product Roadmap and Data Flywheel

The AI Product Roadmap is a strategic tool that outlines the development process of an AI product, starting from problem identification to deployment. It addresses the unique technical challenges and requirements associated with AI-driven products and provides a framework for cross-functional collaboration. There are five key principles that inform the AI Product Roadmap:

1. Define a clear AI vision and strategy: Establish a product vision that aligns with the organization's overall strategy and identifies specific use cases that tackle important problems using machine learning techniques.
2. Focus on user needs and experiences: AI-driven products must satisfy user requirements and enhance their experiences to be successful. Conduct thorough users research and employ user-centered design principles to optimize their satisfaction and adoption. 3. Align product features with AI capabilities: Determine the features and functionality of the product based on the current state and availability of AI technology, balancing ambition with technical feasibility. 4. Embrace iterative development: AI projects are complex and often contain many unknowns. Employ an iterative development process, leveraging continuous feedback and learning to improve

the product quality over time. 5. Measure success with meaningful metrics: Develop Key Performance Indicators (KPIs) that reflect the product's impact on users and the organization's broader strategic objectives.

A successful AI product development process begins with a problem statement, followed by data collection, exploration, feature engineering, model training, evaluation, and deployment. As the product development progresses through these stages, it's essential to ensure the roadmap stays agile, adjusting and iterating on priorities and timelines as required.

While the AI Product Roadmap defines the strategic plan of action, the Data Flywheel concept is pivotal in harnessing the power of data to fuel AI product development efforts. The Data Flywheel is a self-reinforcing cycle where the collection, processing, and utilization of data become more efficient with time and scale, resulting in improved AI performance. The Data Flywheel has four critical components:

1. Data Acquisition: Identify relevant data sources, collect, and store data efficiently for building and training AI models. 2. Data Transformation: Process and structure raw data into a format suitable for machine learning algorithms, employing practices such as data cleaning, normalization, and feature extraction. 3. Data Utilization: Use the transformed data to train and improve machine learning models, deploy them into production, and derive valuable insights that benefit users and the organization. 4. Data Feedback: Gather user feedback and additional data from deployed AI products to inform future iterations and improvements.

Real-world companies have successfully applied these frameworks to build AI-driven solutions. Notable examples include Amazon, which has leveraged its Data Flywheel to optimize its recommendation engine and streamline inventory management, and Tesla, which has used an AI Product Roadmap to navigate the development of its self-driving technology.

In conclusion, the AI Product Roadmap and Data Flywheel frameworks provide a robust foundation for organizations to navigate the complexities of AI product development. Embracing these frameworks helps organizations to align their AI projects with market opportunities and customer needs, leverage the power of data, and drive successful product innovation. As we continue to explore the nuances of abstraction and the myriad ways it shapes our understanding, let's consider how retaining critical information through these frameworks can guide us toward responsible and ethical abstraction practices. By embracing the lessons learned from applying these strategic tools, we can further cultivate our abstraction skills, continuously refining our methods for optimal results in an AI-driven world.

# AI Product Roadmap: Key Principles and Strategies

The first principle to consider while creating an AI product roadmap is establishing a clear vision and setting achievable goals. Articulating the vision for the AI product helps align the entire development team and other stakeholders. The vision should guide the product's evolution, ensuring all efforts maintain a customer-centric focus and contribute to the organization's strategic objectives. This vision will also help in setting measurable short-term and long-term goals based on the desired outcomes, which will serve as milestones in the AI product roadmap.

Next, it is essential to foster cross-functional collaboration and communication, as developing an AI product requires a diverse range of expertise such as data science, engineering, design, and domain knowledge. Organizations should establish a cross-functional product team, encompassing representatives from multiple departments, to ensure seamless collaboration and coverage of all relevant perspectives. Frequent communication with stakeholders enables the up-to-date understanding of their needs and potential challenges. Additionally, this approach promotes collective decision-making, leading to more informed choices throughout development.

Third, incorporating a modular and iterative development approach is indispensable in creating an AI product roadmap. Instead of attempting to build a large-scale, complex AI system in its entirety, product developers should focus on accomplishing smaller, incremental tasks. This enables rapid prototyping, testing, and iteration, ensuring earlier feedback from customers and stakeholders. The iterative approach allows the team to make continuous improvements and refinements to the product, leading to a more fine-tuned and fully-realized AI solution.

To ensure a successful AI product roadmap, flexibility should be embedded into the planning process. The AI landscape is rapidly evolving, which necessitates that organizations remain agile and adaptable. As new data becomes available, insights emerge, and customers' needs change, teams must be prepared to recalibrate the roadmap based on the new information.

Emphasizing flexibility ensures that the product being developed remains relevant and capable of delivering value in a shifting landscape.

For instance, consider the development of an AI-driven customer support chatbot for an e-commerce platform. The project's vision could be to provide real-time, personalized support to customers 24/7, enhancing user satisfaction and increasing the likelihood of repeat purchases. The AI product roadmap would begin with short-term goals, such as developing a proof-of-concept or minimum viable product (MVP) and conducting initial user testing. As customer feedback is collected and assessed, the roadmap could include further refinements in natural language processing capabilities, integrations with other platforms, and automation of additional customer support processes.

In this example, the cross-functional development team would consist of data scientists, software engineers, user experience designers, customer support representatives, and various domain experts. The team would adopt an iterative, modular approach, focusing on developing specific components of the chatbot incrementally to facilitate earlier testing and feedback. Lastly, the roadmap would allow for adjustments based on new data, ensuring that the chatbot continuously evolves and adapts to the rapidly changing customer support landscape.

In conclusion, creating an AI product roadmap demands clarity of vision, an emphasis on collaboration, an iterative development approach, and the readiness to adapt to change. By incorporating these principles and strategies, organizations can successfully chart the course for AI-powered solutions that not only meet but exceed customer expectations. As we proceed through the realm of abstraction and complexity, the following sections of this book will explore more nuanced principles and techniques for grappling with AI product development in a world of increasing interconnectedness and innovation.

## Implementing the AI Product Roadmap: Steps and Best Practices

First and foremost, an AI product roadmap must be structured around a solid understanding of the company's strategic priorities and business objectives. This can be done through a collaborative process between business stakeholders and the AI team, drawing upon their respective areas of expertise to ensure that the roadmap aligns with both the organization's vision and its technical feasibility. Understanding the goals of the business is paramount in steering AI efforts in the right direction, maximizing the return on investment and fostering a culture of innovation within the organization.

Once the strategic priorities have been identified, it is essential to establish a pragmatic and incremental approach to AI development. Instead of pursuing a "moonshot" project that might prove too ambitious, organizations should identify achievable and measurable milestones along the AI product roadmap. These milestones should be focused on delivering tangible benefits to the business, ultimately contributing to the organization's overall objectives and inspiring confidence in the value of AI.

To accomplish these milestones, organizations should adopt a cross - functional and collaborative approach to AI development. This entails assembling a diverse team of experts spanning various domains, such as data science, software engineering, product management, and user experience. By bringing together individuals with complementary skill sets, organizations can ensure that the development process is robust, efficient, and tailored to the specific needs of the business.

In the realm of AI, data reigns supreme. Any AI product roadmap must be underpinned by a solid data strategy that ensures the availability, quality, and relevancy of the data used to train and test AI models. A strong data strategy is also essential for the long - term sustainability of AI products, enabling organizations to continually improve their offerings by leveraging the insights gained from new data sources.

As the AI product roadmap is executed, organizations should foster a culture of learning and experimentation. Given the rapid pace of technological advancements in AI, it is essential that teams continuously expand their knowledge and adopt new techniques to stay ahead of the curve. This can be encouraged through regular knowledge - sharing sessions, workshops, and ongoing professional development opportunities.

Collaboration with external partners, such as universities, research institutions, and other organizations, can also provide valuable opportunities to learn, innovate, and enhance the AI product roadmap. In some cases, these collaborations may lead to the development of AI solutions that possess a competitive edge or are of strategic importance to the organization.

Monitoring progress and assessing the impact of the AI product roadmap is another crucial aspect of its execution. By defining key performance indicators (KPIs) and regularly evaluating the performance of the AI products against these metrics, organizations can ensure that their efforts remain aligned with business objectives and make informed decisions about resource allocation and prioritization.

Constant communication and transparency are essential for maintaining alignment and managing expectations throughout the implementation of the AI product roadmap. By keeping stakeholders informed about the status of milestones, project risks, and developments, organizations can support a culture of innovation and foster a clear vision for the future of AI within the company.

As the AI product roadmap progresses, it is likely that organizations will encounter unforeseen challenges and opportunities. In response to these changing dynamics, companies should remain agile and ready to adapt their AI product roadmap as needed. This may involve revisiting the strategic priorities, reassessing the allocation of resources, and exploring new partnerships or technologies that can enhance the roadmap's impact.

In conclusion, the implementation of an AI product roadmap is a complex and dynamic process, requiring a thoughtful balance of strategic vision, technical expertise, and organizational agility. By embracing a culture of collaboration, learning, and adaptation, organizations can successfully navigate the challenges of AI development and unleash the full potential of this transformative technology. As technology continues to evolve and AI becomes more deeply ingrained in every aspect of our lives, the ability to craft and execute AI product roadmaps will be an invaluable skill for businesses seeking to leverage this powerful force for innovation and growth.

## Data Flywheel Concept: Importance and Benefits for AI Product Development

As with any successful endeavor, the development of an AI product requires a combination of vision, planning, execution, and an abundance of data. Data, often considered the foundation on which AI products are built, plays an essential role in every stage of the development process, from algorithm training to model evaluation. It is arguably the most significant driver of an AI product's ability to learn, adapt, and perform in a manner that adds value to its users. As such, it is vital not to overlook the importance of a data flywheel in the development of AI products.

The data flywheel concept is premised on the idea that, in order to continuously enhance a product's performance, a data-driven feedback loop must be established and perpetuated. At its core, an effective data flywheel consists of four interrelated steps: the collection of data, the analysis of the collected data, making informed decisions based on those analyses, and using the acquired knowledge to gather even more relevant data. The continuous cycle created by this process is the force that drives an AI product's rapid growth and performance.

The importance of a data flywheel cannot be understated. AI-driven products and services rely on access to diverse, high-quality data for their success. Think of it as if you were building a world-class race car - having the best design and engineering team is equally as crucial as having access to the highest quality fuel to propel the car to victory. Data serves as the fuel that powers the AI engine. Inadequate or poorly processed data may severely hamper the performance of the system, impair its ability to provide something of value, and ultimately limit the chances of seeing a return on investment.

Developing an effective data flywheel brings several benefits to the AI product development process. Let's explore these benefits through the lens of a hypothetical health-monitoring wearable device powered by AI algorithms that analyze a user's vital signs to detect abnormalities and alert them to potential health risks.

First and foremost, an efficient data flywheel enables the rapid improvement of algorithms responsible for the device's core function. By continuously gathering data from the wearer's vitals, the wearable can better understand the person's baseline health, detect anomalies, and learn to make more accurate predictions by applying this newly acquired information within the data flywheel. As the device gains access to ever-growing amounts of diverse data, its algorithm becomes increasingly robust and reliable, providing the wearer with increasingly valuable health insights.

Secondly, a well-functioning data flywheel fosters organic and sustainable user engagement. In the context of our health-monitoring wearable, as the algorithm evolves, it becomes increasingly adept at recommending personalized and actionable insights. These recommendations, in turn, lead users to rely more heavily on the wearable, thereby generating even more data for the system to analyze. Consequently, this creates a virtuous cycle of continued improvement and increased user loyalty, driving the product's success and longevity.

Finally, a data flywheel has the potential to unlock new features, products, and even entire markets that may not have been immediately apparent during the initial stages of development. For instance, our wearable device could collect data on users' heart rates during sports, fitness, or recreational activities. As the data flywheel grows, it may eventually uncover correlations between users' vitals and specific activities - information that could be utilized to create new niche features within the device or even entirely new products aimed at specific user segments.

In essence, the data flywheel concept embodies a symbiotic relationship between an AI product's performance and user satisfaction. A well-designed data flywheel generates a continuous cascade of valuable insights, better decision-making, and further opportunities for growth, cementing the AI product's position as an indispensable part of the user's life. By emphasizing the importance and benefits of establishing a data flywheel during AI product development, we can lay the groundwork for a future where AI products not only meet but exceed the needs and expectations of their users, creating lasting value, and continuously unlocking new possibilities in a world that runs on data. And just like a carefully constructed flywheel maintains and magnifies the momentum of the machine it powers, the data flywheel keeps the AI product advancing on the path to success, innovation, and preeminence in an ever-changing digital landscape.

# Building a Data Flywheel: Guidelines and Success Factors

First, it is essential to understand that the foundation of a successful data flywheel is the quality and diversity of data sources. By incorporating a wide variety of data points, organizations can create more robust and accurate AI models. This begins with the careful selection and combination of internal and external data sources, such as customer behavior and preferences, market trends, and industry benchmarks. The more comprehensive and granular the data, the better the insights that can be derived from it.

In addition to data diversity, organizations must ensure data accuracy and quality. This requires implementing systems and processes for data validation, normalization, and cleansing. By eliminating data inconsistencies, errors, and redundancies, organizations can increase the reliability and accuracy of their AI models, enhancing the overall performance of the data flywheel.

Another vital component of building a data flywheel is developing a strong data infrastructure. The volume and velocity of data in modern AI applications necessitate robust, scalable, and flexible infrastructure solutions. This includes the implementation of data warehouses, data lakes, or hybrid solutions that can accommodate growing data volumes while maintaining efficient data processing and storage capabilities. Furthermore, organizations should invest in the integration of advanced analytics and machine learning tools to augment their ability to extract insights from data.

Closely related to data infrastructure is the importance of data governance. To prevent misuse, misinterpretation, or loss of data, organizations must implement robust data access controls and security measures. This includes establishing policies and procedures for data handling, compliance with data protection regulations, and creating a data catalog to track and monitor the lineage and usage of data elements. By implementing sound data governance practices, organizations can protect the integrity of their data assets and ensure that the data flywheel can function effectively.

Equally important as the technical aspects of building a data flywheel is the organizational culture, mindset, and skillset necessary for its success. To foster a data - driven culture and embrace the data flywheel concept, organizations must cultivate a mentality of continuous learning and improvement. By investing in their talent pool and ensuring that employees possess the necessary skills to work with data, organizations can maximize the value derived from the data flywheel. This includes building a cross - functional team of experts, such as data scientists, data engineers, and domain experts, who can collaborate on data - driven projects and facilitate rapid iteration and experimentation.

Ultimately, the key to successfully building a data flywheel is understanding how to translate data into actionable insights and feedback loops that drive continuous improvement. For instance, consider an e - commerce platform that collects customer browsing and purchase data. By analyzing this data and identifying patterns in customer preferences and behavior, the platform can continuously refine its recommendation algorithms and create a more personalized shopping experience. This customization results in increased customer engagement and loyalty, which in turn generates more data to fuel the data flywheel and sustain its momentum.

Innovation and adaptability are essential in successfully harnessing the power of the data flywheel. As AI technologies and data science methodologies continue to evolve, organizations must remain agile in embracing new approaches to unlock the full potential of the data flywheel. A continuous commitment to refining, enhancing, and expanding the scope of the data flywheel will ensure that organizations can not only reap the immediate benefits of data - driven decision - making but also lay the foundation for long - term, sustainable growth.

To conclude, building a data flywheel requires a confluence of technical and organizational factors, including data quality and diversity, robust infrastructure and governance, and a data - driven culture that fosters continuous learning and improvement. By realizing the potential of the data flywheel, AI product development can be transformed, enabling organizations to achieve lasting competitive advantage and drive growth in an increasingly data-driven world. As we continue to explore the principles and strategies of AI product roadmaps, the iterative and dynamic nature of the data flywheel sets the stage for an exciting journey ahead.

## Case Studies: Real - world Applications of AI Product Roadmap and Data Flywheel

First, let us consider a multinational retail corporation that embarked on an ambitious journey to revolutionize its supply chain operations using AI - powered predictive analytics. To achieve this vision, the company developed an AI product roadmap that outlined their strategic objectives, technical components, and a phased delivery plan. This roadmap guided the development and implementation of machine learning models for inventory optimization and demand forecasting, leading to significant reductions in stockouts and overstock situations.

To further advance in this domain and utilize the power of data, the company built a data flywheel in which successive iterations of the AI models were continually trained and improved using the supply chain data. By feeding back the outputs of the models into the training process, the company was able to create a virtuous cycle where the AI algorithms became more accurate and efficient with each iteration. This systematic approach not only drove massive operational improvements but also established the organization as an industry leader in AI-driven supply chain management.

Next, let's look at an innovative healthcare technology start-up that developed an AI-powered diagnostic tool for early detection of certain medical conditions using image recognition algorithms. The development team created an AI product roadmap that outlined the stages of product development, from the initial research and data collection to model training, validation, and deployment. The roadmap also identified key risks and dependencies, such as securing regulatory approvals and overcoming data privacy concerns, thereby enabling the team to proactively address potential challenges.

The start-up's data flywheel harnessed the power of a vast database of anonymized medical images, which continually expanded as new images were added and used to enhance the diagnostic capabilities of the AI model. As healthcare providers worldwide adopted the tool, the data flywheel effect became even more pronounced, leading to a significant improvement in diagnostic accuracy over time.

Finally, let us consider a mid-sized financial services firm that sought to improve its customer service through AI-driven chatbot technology. The firm established an AI product roadmap that identified the essential components, such as natural language processing algorithms, training datasets, and user interface design, as well as key project milestones and deliverables. The AI product roadmap kept the team aligned and focused on the most critical tasks, ultimately leading to a chatbot that exceeded both internal and customer expectations.

As the chatbot began handling an increasing number of customer inquiries, the company saw an opportunity to create a data flywheel that would enhance the AI model's performance. They set up a mechanism to automatically incorporate anonymized chat transcripts into the model's training data, effectively using customer interactions to improve the chatbot's capabilities over time. This data flywheel accelerated the chatbot's ability to respond accurately to a broader range of customer inquiries, further elevating its value to the organization.

These case studies demonstrate the transformative potential of AI when guided by a well-structured product roadmap and reinforced through a data flywheel mechanism. The key takeaway is that strategic planning, combined with a systematic approach to capitalizing on data feedback loops, can pave the way for considerable advancements in AI projects across diverse industries.

As we move forward, let us bear in mind the significance of context awareness and nuanced thinking when designing AI products and systems. By doing so, we can harness the power of abstraction while ensuring that our AI initiatives yield optimal results without compromising their ethical integrity or relevance to real-world challenges.

# Chapter 7

# Responsible Abstraction: Bias, Ethics, and the Importance of Inclusivity

Responsible abstraction is essential for engaging with the increasingly complex world we live in, where streamlining information and processes is not only beneficial but can be the difference between success and failure. However, the act of abstracting itself can introduce a range of unintended consequences when it comes to bias, ethics, and inclusivity. The responsibility lies with each individual and organization to approach abstraction with mindfulness and ensure that the practices they employ are equal, fair, and nondiscriminatory.

We often operate with a range of cognitive biases that can influence our decision-making process. Many of these, such as anchoring, availability heuristic, and confirmation bias, can impact the way we abstract information. As a result, it can lead to an incomplete or incorrect understanding of a concept or situation. One of the most concerning aspects of this biased abstraction is the potential for perpetuating stereotypes, discrimination, and social injustices. When grounding our abstractions on biased assumptions, we risk perpetuating inaccurate and potentially harmful perspectives.

Take, for example, the development of facial recognition algorithms. During the abstraction process, we extract essential features of a face and discard irrelevant details. However, if our choice of essential features is biased towards a particular race or gender, the facial recognition algorithms may perform poorly on individuals from underrepresented groups. In some cases, these disparities in performance may have real-world consequences; for example, the wrongful arrest and conviction due to misidentification of a person of color by a biased facial recognition system. Accordingly, it is of utmost importance for those involved in such projects to be aware of potential biases within their abstract thinking and take active steps to mitigate them.

In parallel with addressing biases, responsible abstraction involves considering the ethical implications of simplifying complex systems. This entails evaluating the potential consequences of our choices on various stakeholders, especially the unintended ones. By doing this, we can make informed decisions about how and what to abstract, ensuring that we balance the need for simplicity with the ethical considerations of the abstraction process. For instance, when modeling the spread of an infectious disease, one must weigh the potential benefits of simplification, such as increased computational efficiency, against the distorting effects of those simplifications on the system's behavior and its implications on the treatment and prevention efforts.

One crucial aspect of responsible abstraction is the emphasis on inclusivity. Abstract thinking must reflect the diversity of our world and avoid undue generalizations that may overlook the needs and perspectives of minority populations. By intentionally incorporating different viewpoints, particularly those that are often marginalized, we can build more accurate, useful, and equitable abstractions that serve the greater good.

For instance, when designing a public transportation system for a city, it is essential to understand the travel needs, patterns, and preferences of various demographic groups. An abstract model that fails to account for differences in mobility for people with disabilities or considers accessibility for lower-income populations can limit the capacity of the public transit system to serve everyone effectively. Through purposeful abstraction tailoring, taking into account the needs and perspectives of underrepresented groups becomes integral to the design process.

To practice responsible abstraction, it is crucial to develop an awareness of biases that may be influencing one's reasoning and remain vigilant of ethical considerations surrounding the choices made during the abstraction process. By questioning assumptions, avoiding false dichotomies, and tailoring abstractions to suit the needs of various stakeholders, one can create an inclusive and ethically grounded abstraction strategy.

But why stop there? The journey of responsible abstraction should be considered an ongoing process of continuous improvement. As the world evolves, so too does our understanding of the various systems that comprise it, providing ample opportunities to refine and enhance our abstractions. By embracing curiosity, humility, and introspection, we can adapt, learn, and grow in our efforts to create more equitable, inclusive, and ethically responsible abstractions.

As we venture forth into the complex web of abstract representations that shape our decisions, let us remember in each step to appraise the implications of our actions. By doing so, we can contribute to a more inclusive and just world, where abstraction becomes a tool to address the challenges we face rather than exacerbate them.

## Understanding Bias in Abstraction: Recognizing Unconscious Preferences and Misrepresentations

One of the fundamental aspects of abstraction is the creation of mental models, which are simplified representations of complex entities or processes. While mental models are useful in making sense of the world, they can also give rise to certain biases that result from our unconscious preferences and misrepresentations. Among these biases, the most pervasive one is confirmation bias, which refers to the tendency to seek, interpret and focus on information that confirms one's pre - existing beliefs and expectations while ignoring or downplaying contradictory evidence.

Consider, for example, a software engineer tasked with abstracting a large - scale software system's functionality. The engineer might be naturally inclined to favor designs and architectures they have successfully used in the past, potentially disregarding novel approaches that might be better suited to the problem at hand. Their confirmation bias, in this case, might lead them to create an abstraction that over - emphasizes the relevance of familiar patterns while neglecting other essential aspects of the system. As a result, the abstraction may not accurately represent the complexities of the software system and can inadvertently narrow the design space, stifling innovation.

Another manifestation of bias in abstraction is the availability heuristic, which refers to the cognitive strategy of relying on the most readily available, recent, or memorable information when making judgments or decisions. When abstracting complex ideas or systems, we might fall prey to the availability heuristic by inadvertently emphasizing aspects that are most salient or have been encountered most recently in our experience. This can lead to distorted representations that overstate the importance of certain details while downplaying or omitting others that might be crucial.

For instance, consider a product manager designing an abstraction of a customer segmentation model. They are likely to overemphasize recent customer interactions or high-profile clients in their abstraction, potentially overlooking other, more representative trends that could have a greater impact on the product's success. In this case, the availability heuristic can skew the abstraction towards a less accurate representation of customer preferences, which can ultimately hamper the effectiveness of the product.

While it is unrealistic to expect complete impartiality in abstract thinking, being mindful of the various ways biases can infiltrate our mental models is an essential first step towards mitigating their impact. To counter these biases, it is important to maintain an open and inquisitive mind, questioning our assumptions, and actively seeking alternative perspectives that challenge our preconceived ideas. In the context of abstraction, this might involve seeking input from diverse stakeholders, comparing multiple abstractions of the same concept, or soliciting feedback from colleagues with different backgrounds and expertise.

Additionally, embracing an iterative approach to abstraction can help us recognize and rectify biases that emerge during the abstraction process. By revisiting and refining our abstractions, we can become more sensitive to the presence of biases and take corrective measures as needed. As we iterate through this process, we are likely to develop cognitive flexibility, enabling us to pivot our abstractions when faced with novel information or changing circumstances.

## Ethical Considerations in Abstraction: Balancing Simplification and Fairness

Consider, for example, the symbolic system of language. Words themselves are abstractions, formed by compressing a vast array of sensations, experiences, and emotions into a limited set of symbols. Yet, as we well know, language, especially in its written form, can be a double - edged sword, capable of both illuminating and obfuscating understanding. When we choose words, we are engaged in a process of abstraction, and our choice has consequences for both clarity and fairness. Is it ethical, for instance, to use the word "primitive" to describe a pre - industrial society, even if that term captures some aspects of its technological situation, when it may also perpetuate stereotypes about the capabilities and worth of its members?

When tackling problems in the realm of artificial intelligence, abstraction becomes even more critical and ethically challenging. Machine learning algorithms rely upon abstraction to analyze data, seeking out patterns among countless variables and learning to discern what is significant from what is mere noise. But as these algorithms gain increasing influence over our lives, from predictive policing to job candidate selection to medical diagnoses, we must be profoundly attentive to how the abstractions they employ might inadvertently skew results or perpetuate biases. Otherwise, without proper guidance, the AI might unintentionally adopt biased abstractions that reinforce existing social inequalities and perpetuate harmful stereotypes.

The renowned concept of the trolley problem can also shed light on the ethical dimensions of abstraction. This famous ethical dilemma presents a choice between diverting a runaway trolley to a track where it would kill one person or allowing it to continue on its course where it would kill five others. As a purely abstract problem, the trolley dilemma seems to offer a straightforward choice that rests on numeric calculations: one life versus five. However, when confronted with real-life situations involving complex human emotions and relationships, the same trolley problem becomes far less easily resolvable. We are then forced to contend with issues such as the value of individual lives against the collective good, responsibility and agency, or situational context - considerations that defy simple quantification.

To ensure the ethical use of abstraction, we must first recognize that our responsibility extends beyond selecting the appropriate level of abstraction. We must also be highly conscious of the aspect of value biases that may inadvertently seep into our abstract models. This consciousness begins by acknowledging that the process of abstraction, while aiming for the "truth," is ultimately shaped by human subjectivities, beliefs, and values. By embracing this reality, we can better equip ourselves to scrutinize our own abstractions to identify and minimize potential biases.

One way to achieve this is by involving a diverse set of perspectives in the abstraction process, bringing together individuals from a variety of backgrounds, cultures, and fields of expertise. This collaborative approach can help to challenge assumptions, reveal blind spots, and foster richer and more ethically responsible abstractions that consider a broader range of perspectives and interests.

Moreover, the ethical practice of abstraction demands constant vigilance, as the process is neither static nor final. Just as the world around us evolves, so too must our abstractions. We should continuously examine, refine, and reassess our methods of abstraction, holding ourselves accountable for their results, and being open to revising them when they are found wanting. Furthermore, we should strive for transparency in our practices. By making the process and assumptions underlying our abstractions explicit, we encourage critical scrutiny and facilitate the collective pursuit of ethical and effective abstraction.

In conclusion, the art of abstraction is an essential tool for managing complexity, empowering us to discern patterns, capture information, and think critically about the world around us. However, as with any powerful tool, wielding abstraction ethically requires a constant awareness of the potential pitfalls and distortions that may accompany the simplification process. By fostering an inclusive, transparent, and self-reflective practice, we can navigate the intricate balance between simplification and fairness, ultimately elevating our capacity for understanding and creating solutions that respect the rich tapestry of human experiences. As we proceed to the next phase of our exploration, we must bear in mind the critical importance of context-dependence in abstract thinking, and continually strive to hone our skill in selecting the appropriate level of abstraction that encapsulates both the salient and the subtle elements of the phenomena we seek to comprehend.

## Inclusivity in Abstract Thinking: Promoting Diversity and Representation

As we delve into the labyrinthine world of abstraction - a journey filled with trials and tribulations - it is imperative to acknowledge and embrace the significance of diversity and representation. While minds may soar through the skies of abstraction, we must remain grounded in the reality that our ideas and thoughts are influenced by our unique circumstances, experiences, and backgrounds. These influences are present even in our higher-order thinking, shaping and refining our abstract reasoning, reflecting an ever-changing tapestry of lived human experience, with each new thread woven contributing to the pattern. By actively promoting diversity and representation in our abstract thinking, the tapestry becomes more vibrant, resilient, and, most importantly, enriched.

Consider a team of software engineers tasked with designing an AI-based natural language processing algorithm for a multinational company. The engineers, though skilled and trained in the various art forms of abstraction, come from a predominantly uniform cultural background. As a result, the AI system they create is narrow-minded-it accurately processes the grammar and idioms common to their shared culture but fails miserably when engaging users from other linguistic backgrounds.

This unfortunate tale illustrates the critical need for inclusivity in abstract thinking. By recognizing limitations and blind spots in our approaches, we can facilitate an environment where diverse perspectives can flourish, in which people from various cultures, beliefs, and genders can construct an ecosystem of ideas that sparks an explosion of creativity and innovation. Inclusivity in abstract thinking does not merely enhance the collective wisdom of groups and organizations but amplifies the imaginative prowess and analytical abilities of each individual.

One key strategy to promoting diversity and representation in abstraction is to actively seek out and welcome perspectives that challenge one's assumptions. By broadening the array of experiences and viewpoints available, we foster an environment where individuals can perceive new dimensions and trajectories that might not have emerged otherwise. Encourage dialogue, appreciate alternative viewpoints, and collaboratively question established norms. An atmosphere of healthy intellectual curiosity is one hallmark of a diverse and inclusive abstract thinking process.

However, championing diversity and representation involves more than merely assembling a 'mosaic' of unique individuals with different viewpoints; it requires continuous effort to invest in understanding the context, background, and experiences that inform these perspectives. One way to achieve this is to engage in cultural and interdisciplinary exploration. Familiarize yourself with approaches from different disciplines, immerse yourself in unfamiliar cultural contexts, and challenge your preconceptions by learning to see the world through others' eyes. By immersing in new experiences, you will become more adept at perceiving the intricacies and subtleties that characterize others' thought processes, enriching your own abstract thinking abilities in turn.

Another essential component of promoting diversity and representation in abstraction is cultivating empathy. The ability to appreciate and value others' viewpoints is indispensable when aiming to elevate abstract thinking. Empathy allows us to reimagine our perceptions of problems and solutions, enabling the birth of new ideas that manage complexity with greater dexterity. This emotional intelligence endows abstract thinkers with an additional layer of nuance, allowing them to navigate the shifting winds of cognition more effectively.

In conclusion, the chimerical art of abstraction transcends the confines of rigid rationality and sterile logic. It is an intricate dance on the edge of chaos and order, fueled and shaped by the multitude of experiences, perceptions, and emotions that color our human existence. By actively fostering diversity and representation in our abstract thinking and surrounding ourselves with a kaleidoscope of viewpoints, experiences, and ideas, we can achieve a level of mental sophistication and agility that far surpasses what we could attain on our own. As we turn the page to explore the significance of challenging assumptions, breaking down false dichotomies, and tailoring abstractions to their specific contexts, let us remember that inclusivity is not merely an ideal to strive for - it is a potent instrument of transformation that can elevate our abstract reasoning to unparalleled heights. So let us weave the tapestry of abstraction, united by a shared determination to explore and celebrate the boundless expanse of human insight.

## Developing Guidelines for Responsible Abstraction: Best Practices and Practical Solutions

Developing guidelines for responsible abstraction entails creating a set of best practices and practical solutions that help practitioners and organizations generate accurate and representative models without sacrificing critical information. Real-world decision-making is often multifaceted, requiring abstractions that capture and maintain important details while simplifying the complexity underlying real-world situations and systems. To achieve responsible abstraction, it is essential to adopt a disciplined approach that addresses common issues such as unconscious biases, oversimplification, and misrepresentations that can lead to unfair or inaccurate outcomes.

Firstly, one must establish the purpose and boundaries of the abstraction. This involves outlining the specific problem the abstraction is intended to solve and determining which elements of the system are essential for accurately addressing the issue. Clarifying the objective serves as a foundation upon which to build accurate and useful abstractions while preventing unnecessary complexity.

Next, identifying and retaining essential details is critical. When creating an abstraction, it can be tempting to generalize too much or strip away elements that seem insignificant at first glance. To avoid this, focus on the characteristics that truly matter to the problem at hand. For example, in a software system, understanding the interactions between components might be the key to understanding system behavior, while other elements could be abstracted away. Maintaining the fine balance between simplification and retention of critical details is an art, one which requires keen observation and constantly reflecting upon the relevance and significance of various components.

Inclusivity is another important aspect of responsible abstraction. When creating models or building systems, it is vital to consider the diverse perspectives and experiences of stakeholders. Abstraction should not lead to the marginalization or exclusion of any demographic group. Practitioners must strive to counteract any unconscious biases that can creep into the abstraction process and be aware of how their model or system may impact different groups. Collaborative approaches involving diverse teams can provide an opportunity to exchange perspectives and challenge assumptions, leading to more robust and ethically sound outcomes.

Establishing an iterative feedback process helps refine ongoing abstractions by testing its accuracy or efficacy over time. Gathering user feedback, conducting experiments, or simulating scenarios allows practitioners to rapidly identify any errors or discrepancies. The iterative process allows abstractions to be improved and adjusted continuously as new information, perspectives, or challenges emerge, resulting in a more accurate representation and better overall performance.

Responsible abstraction also involves managing the trade-off between precision and generalization. While abstractions are meant to simplify complex concepts, the aim should be to provide a concise and accurate representation without losing essential context. Practitioners should always ensure that their abstractions do not compromise the fidelity of the model to such an extent that it loses relevance or fails to address underlying issues.

Transparency and communication are crucial for responsible abstraction, especially when presenting results or leveraging abstractions for decision-making. Clearly documenting the assumptions, limitations, and context of the abstraction promotes understanding and enables users to apply the knowledge in a responsible manner. Furthermore, encouraging open dialogue around the impacts of the abstraction fosters trust and creates a culture of continuous learning.

To evoke a vivid example, let's consider an autonomous vehicle's design process. The development team is tasked with creating an abstraction that represents the terrain and environment of the vehicle's operational domain. A responsible abstraction should capture essential elements such as road topology, traffic patterns, pedestrian priority zones, and ecological constraints. However, it must do so without succumbing to oversimplification or introducing system biases towards certain geographies or road users. The ongoing iterative process of refining the abstraction, incorporating stakeholder feedback, and documenting the limitations ensures a fair and accurate representation, which ultimately contributes to the safety and efficiency of the autonomous vehicle.

In conclusion, developing guidelines for responsible abstraction neither has concrete steps nor rigid rules; it is an art that relies on continuous reflection and refinement. It requires attention to detail, recognizing and embracing diversity, and being open to collaboration and learning. Delivering responsible abstractions is essential for ethically sound decisions, fostering trust in outcomes, and facilitating progress across various domains. As the penultimate tip of the abstraction iceberg surfaces, we must not forget to continue evaluating and polishing our abstraction skills - for it is the ongoing journey of mastery that propels personal and professional growth.

# Chapter 8

# Retaining Critical Information: Balancing Abstraction with Essential Details

In our relentless pursuit of understanding and managing the complexity of the world, we often find ourselves wielding the powerful double-edged sword of abstraction. By discarding superfluous details and identifying shared structures, we can take a more efficient and general view of problems, making them more easily solvable. However, the risk of going too far in simplification is always lurking, which could lead to an impoverished understanding, biased conclusions, and even outright falsehoods. To unlock the true potential of abstraction, it is necessary to master the art of retaining critical information while discarding the rest.

Consider the world of mapmaking. Cartographers have long grappled with the problem of abstraction, balancing accuracy and detail with simplicity and usability. A map too drowned in detail becomes illegible, while one with too much information omitted risks being misleading, or worse, useless altogether.

Let us take an example from the world of finance: an organization attempting to create a risk modeling framework to assess their investment portfolio. The ultimate goals are to accurately estimate the probability and impact of various market events or policy changes. Here, striking the balance between abstraction and retaining critical information is both an art and a science.

To start, one must identify the essential information required. In this case, key factors could include macroeconomic indicators, relevant industry trends, the financial health of companies in the portfolio, policy stability, and more. Consciously prioritizing which aspects are truly critical to the analysis can be an invaluable exercise in clarifying thinking and preventing over - abstraction.

Secondly, integrating multiple perspectives and cross-functional expertise is crucial for avoiding potential biases and oversights. Engaging with finance experts, data scientists, industry insiders, and economists could ensure the inclusion of essential details that might have otherwise been overlooked.

Another essential practice for retaining crucial information is to regularly challenge and revise assumptions. As with any abstraction process, working with risk modeling frameworks requires taking a stance on what is important and what can be discarded. However, even well - informed stances can be mistaken or obsolete as realities change. In this process, it is crucial to be humble and open to the possibility that one's convictions might be less ironclad than one thought.

A practical way to balance abstraction with retaining essential information is to adopt an iterative approach. As new complexities or unforeseen interactions emerge, the models can be updated and refined. Borrowing from the world of agile methodologies, this involves constantly reassessing, reevaluating, and adapting the initial abstraction frame while still maintaining a manageable and functional structure.

One final piece of advice in retaining critical information is to maintain a connection with the real world as much as possible. Over - reliance on theoretical constructs and abstract simulations can lead to a disconnect from ground realities. Regularly seeking feedback from those who are directly impacted by your abstracted models, or even involving them in the process, can ensure that truly essential information is preserved.

However, it would be naive to assume that retaining critical information can be distilled into a straightforward procedure with clear - cut rules. As with any art, mastering the balance between abstraction and the preservation of essential details requires practice, experience, and intuition. Developing this balance is, in many ways, the core challenge of any and all abstraction endeavors.

One must walk the razor's edge between understanding and oversimplification, relying on both intellectual acumen and humble self-awareness to navigate its dangers. As we venture further into the complexities of our world, we will be better equipped to make decisions, solve problems, and grasp the fundamental nature of things if we face the task with a nuanced, context-aware, and critical mindset.

Thus, a truly adept practitioner of abstraction does not merely wield a powerful tool; they wield a finely tuned instrument, carefully and gracefully striking the delicate balance between simplicity and richness, between discarding the noise and preserving the signal. In doing so, they are poised to unlock the vast potential of abstraction, simultaneously managing complexity and embracing the full depth and wonder of the world around them.

## Introduction to Retaining Critical Information in Abstraction

At the heart of abstraction lies the act of traversing between the specific and the general, navigating from the concrete to the abstract, while identifying and retaining the information that truly matters. We will explore this journey through a lens of storytelling and examples that illustrate the importance of retaining critical information in various domains of human endeavor.

Imagine, for instance, being tasked with the responsibility of redesigning a disaster relief system. This involves taking stock of the many complex, interrelated components of relief infrastructures and distilling them into patterns that can be simplified and reorganized in a more efficient manner. While pursuing such abstraction, the critical detail that must be retained is the human impact. Ultimately, a success in this realm of disaster relief hinges almost entirely upon the capacity to make a difference in the lives of those affected. In the course of abstracting, it is essential to never lose sight of this fact as losing track of this would render the entire effort futile and hollow.

Another example of retaining critical information in abstraction can be seen in the discipline of healthcare, specifically in medical diagnosis and decision-making processes. As medical professionals simplify medical symptoms and signs into patterns and diagnoses, a single overlooked detail could mean the difference between life and death. In such situations, the abstraction process seldom operates in a vacuum, and it is imperative that the abstraction is calibrated to ensure that essential details consistently inform diagnostic decisions.

Retaining critical information during abstraction extends into the domain of communications. A diplomat engages in a delicate dance of abstraction when they summarize a lengthy and nuanced negotiation in a few paragraphs of a press release. In this case, the essential details include the key points of agreement or disagreement. To capture these key points, while still preserving the delicacies of diplomacy, one must strike a fine balance between expression and obfuscation, between clarity and subtlety, all without losing the essential meaning behind the scenes.

In the sphere of scientific research, retaining critical information in the process of abstraction involves parsing through reams of data to find the most significant and relevant findings to develop a hypothesis or bolster an argument. It is the skill of sifting through the chaff to find the wheat that genuinely advances human knowledge. This skill is essential, as oversimplification or the exclusion of relevant data can lead to erroneous conclusions and hamper scientific progress. It is, therefore, crucial that researchers hone their capacity to focus on the critical elements while engaging in abstraction, resulting in more accurate and insightful findings.

All of these examples emphasize the need to stay mindful of the purpose for which we are abstracting. Abstraction without purpose or direction can quickly degenerate into a muddle of simplifications that fail to illuminate or provide insights into complexities. Much like a skilled sailor navigates the treacherous high seas, maintaining a consistent bearing towards their intended destination, so also must we approach abstraction with a clear sense of direction.

As we explore this vital skill of retaining critical information in abstraction further, we will learn techniques and strategies honed from various fields as practical examples, showing both the benefits and challenges of this elusive cognitive art form. And as we sail on the ocean of abstraction, we must never forget to keep our eyes on the horizon, constantly attuned to the critical details that light the way to our destination.

## Identifying Essential Details and Recognizing Superfluous Information

Let's consider an example of designing a public transportation application. A user needs to know the shortest route or quickest time to their desired destination, but they do not need to be constantly informed of every single stop the bus makes, or the color of the bus. In this case, the essential details are the origin and destination, the time it will take, and applicable transfers, while the superfluous information includes the bus ID numbers and traffic light patterns.

It is the discerning eye of the abstracter that unearths the essence of a problem and discards the excess. Many methods and frameworks can aid us in this pursuit, such as the Five Ws and How method, wherein we inquire: What, Who, Where, When, Why, and How? These questions illuminate the critical elements without the fog of irrelevancies.

For a more technical example, let us examine the development of effective data models for a machine learning algorithm. An essential detail in this context would be the data trends correlated with the predicted outcome, whereas superfluous information might be the color of an unrelated datapoint. Unnecessary complexity may lead to overfitting, poor algorithm performance, or difficulty in interpretation.

Perhaps the most classical exemplar of abstraction can be found in mathematics, where mathematicians have long sought patterns that pervade across seemingly disparate realms. The identification of essential details becomes paramount as we strip away non-essential minutiae to uncover core principles. A deceptively simple yet elegant example lies in the Fibonacci sequence, where we abstract the sum of the previous two numbers in the sequence without concerning ourselves with the individuality of the numbers at each step.

The perils of failing to identify essential details or ignoring superfluous information are manifold; undeniably, we have all experienced the frustration of a poorly designed user interface bogged down with excess buttons and features or found an alarm clock that requires three hands to set the time. These are manifestations of abstraction gone awry - systems and products that lose sight of their purpose due to a lack of discernment for essentiality.

This discernment can be seen as an intellectual dance, a fluid and reflexive examination of our underlying assumptions, implicit biases, and cultural contexts. Engaging in this dance requires not only cognitive flexibility but also humility, for it is in the recognition of our blind spots and fallacies that we can aspire to a deeper understanding of abstraction.

Honoring the imperative of essential details in abstraction is as much an art as it is a science; it requires both logical analysis and creative synthesis. We must wield a scalpel of precision yet not at the cost of richness and diversity. As we continue our journey into balancing simplification with retaining essential details, we will explore best practices and practical solutions, venturing into the realms of ethics, inclusivity, and continuous improvement - uncharted territories where abstraction serves as our compass.

## Striking the Balance: Techniques for Maintaining Essential Details while Abstracting

One technique for striking this balance is the "zoom in, zoom out" approach. This involves evaluating a problem or system at multiple levels of granularity, shifting focus periodically between a high - level, abstract representation and a more detailed view of its constituent components. By regularly adjusting the level of abstraction, one can better appreciate the subtleties and dependencies that exist within the system and identify essential details that might otherwise be overlooked.

Consider, for example, a software application that is built using a combination of modular and functional abstraction. At a high level, the application can be conceptualized as a collection of interacting modules that each serve a specific purpose. This modular view allows for easier understanding of the overall architecture and facilitates meaningful discussions about its design. However, to ensure that important details are not lost, one must periodically "zoom in" and examine the specific functions and algorithms employed by each module. This "zoomed in" view provides a more granular perspective on how the modules work together to achieve their intended outcomes, enabling the team to maintain essential details while still taking advantage of the benefits of abstraction.

Another technique for striking the balance between abstraction and retention of essential details is the use of analogies and metaphors. By relating complex concepts to simpler, more familiar ones, analogies can help in developing a deeper understanding of the intricacies of a system without losing sight of its critical components. However, it is important to choose the appropriate analogy or metaphor to ensure its relevance and effectiveness in conveying the intended information.

Take, for instance, the process of designing an autonomous vehicle. A physical abstraction of the vehicle's components can be represented using the metaphor of a human body. In this analogy, the vehicle's various sensors serve as its eyes and ears, its central processing unit as its brain, and its actuators as its limbs. While this metaphor simplifies the complex system, it also ensures that essential details such as the importance of communication between the sensors, processing unit, and actuators are not lost in the abstraction process.

A third technique for maintaining essential details while abstracting involves continuous feedback loops and iterative refinement. By collecting feedback on the abstraction process and its resulting simplifications, individuals and teams can better identify critical details that may have been inadvertently discarded. This feedback can then be used to revise the abstraction, making it more accurate and comprehensive while still remaining accessible and understandable.

In the context of product development, these feedback loops could involve regular presentations of design decisions and their corresponding abstractions to stakeholders. These presentations not only provide an opportunity to gather feedback but also ensure that essential details are retained and communicated effectively.

Finally, one must cultivate a mindset of humility and curiosity to effectively balance abstraction and retention of essential details. Recognizing that no abstraction is perfect and that it might not capture all relevant information encourages us to ask probing questions, challenge our assumptions, and seek out alternative perspectives that might reveal essential details that were previously obscured. This mindset also motivates us to remain open to new approaches and techniques in abstraction, continually expanding our toolbox and refining our ability to distill complex systems into more manageable representations.

## Avoiding Oversimplification and Overgeneralization: Common Mistakes and Solutions

In our quest for abstraction, we must remain mindful of the age-old proverb warning us not to view things "as a hammer, to which everything looks like a nail." When enchanted by the power and elegance of a particular abstraction, we might unknowingly disregard the nuances and complexities of a problem. One prime example is the way in which early economists modeled the behavior of consumers using the concept of a rational, utility-maximizing agent. While powerful and insightful, this abstraction glossed over the myriad of psychological and social factors that govern consumer behavior. Consequently, the predictions based on these simplifications often fell short of reality.

Another common pitfall in the process of abstraction is selecting irrelevant details at the expense of essential ones. For instance, when designing an autonomous vehicle, the size, shape, and weight of the tires are critical details. Still, tire tread design may not be as crucial for building a functionally abstract model, including the effects of variable road conditions or considering battery capacity. By retaining tire tread design at the cost of more critical aspects, the abstraction misses the mark and compromises its utility.

So how can we avoid these mistakes in our pursuit of the perfect abstraction?

In order to avoid oversimplification, we suggest adopting the following practices:

1. Embrace and respect the complexity of the problem domain. Recognize that certain problems inherently possess intricate details and nuances that cannot be trivialized without sacrificing the ability to obtain meaningful solutions.

2. Employ iterative refinement, reconstructing the abstraction by continuously exploring it, scrutinizing its shortcomings, and incorporating feedback from experts and users to progressively refine it. As aerospace engineer Theodore von Kármán aptly put it, "Our knowledge can only be finite, while our ignorance must necessarily be infinite."

3. Utilize cross-domain learning, infusing the abstraction process with insights gained from experience in other domains. By refining our

understanding and interpretation of the world, we broaden our horizons, building a more resilient framework for abstract thinking.

To avoid overgeneralization, consider the following guidelines:

1. Acknowledge the limits of your abstraction. No matter how well-crafted, every abstraction comes with a set of assumptions and boundaries. Be vigilant in identifying these constraints and appropriately qualifying conclusions drawn from the abstraction.

2. Employ context-awareness to ensure that the abstraction is well-suited for the particular set of circumstances that you are faced with. As the great statistician George E.P. Box said, "All models are wrong, but some are useful." By incorporating context-specific factors, we can select the best-fitting abstraction for the task at hand.

3. Seek out assumptions lying behind abstractions and actively question their validity. Uncritical adoption of assumptions may obscure essential details and open the door to generalizations that fail in practice.

4. Lastly, foster diversity, openness, and curiosity in the design process. Creating a safe environment that encourages candid feedback and alternative viewpoints can help uncover potential supports and challenges that a single perspective might miss.

In a world teeming with complexity, striving to adopt the appropriate level of abstraction presents a delicate balance between embracing elegance and avoiding the pitfalls of oversimplification. By drawing on the outlined practices, we grow our capacity to engage in mindful abstraction that not only simplifies but preserves the essence of the problem, empowering us to craft innovative, efficient, and ethically sound solutions.

## Retention of Diversity and Inclusion Indicators in Abstraction Processes

Consider, for example, the process of developing a statistical model to forecast job market trends. One common method might include creating categories, such as age, gender, socio-economic status, and education level. While these categories can indeed help paint a clearer picture of the labor market dynamics, they might not encompass the whole spectrum of diversity that exists among job-seeking individuals. By abstracting away the more nuanced details like sexual orientation, ethnicity, and cognitive or physical disability, we may inadvertently perpetuate existing biases and disparities.

In the context of artificial intelligence, for instance, this negligence can have far-reaching implications. If machine learning models are trained on incomplete or biased data, they will invariably perpetuate or amplify these biases in their outcomes, leading to negative consequences for marginalized and underrepresented groups. We have already seen the consequences of such biases in controversial facial recognition technologies, which tend to produce higher error rates for people with darker skin tones.

To avoid such pitfalls, it is crucial to incorporate diversity and inclusion indicators in the abstraction process, beginning with the identification of which aspects are relevant and essential to understanding and solving a specific problem. This may involve revisiting existing categories and assumptions to evaluate whether they accurately and comprehensively characterize the underlying dynamics. It is also important to remain open to the possibility of identifying new dimensions that were previously overlooked, even if they may complicate the abstraction process.

An important example of making this conscious effort toward inclusive abstraction can be drawn from the domain of healthcare. Ensuring that medical research trials consider a diverse range of participants, including those from different racial and ethnic backgrounds, helps in developing treatments that would be efficacious for a wider population. By maintaining these diversity indicators in study designs and models, researchers can work toward more equitable healthcare outcomes.

In practice, incorporating diversity and inclusion indicators in abstraction processes also means embracing inclusive team dynamics. Engaging in open dialogues and discussions, fostering collaboration and consensus-building, and encouraging team members to reframe problems with an emphasis on retaining diversity and inclusion can promote a more comprehensive approach to matters at hand.

Moreover, it is crucial to remain vigilant against overgeneralizations, which can easily arise with the simplification of complex issues. By continually reevaluating abstractions and their implications, stakeholders can hold themselves accountable for considering the full range of perspectives that warrant attention.

In conclusion, as we navigate the intricate terrain of abstraction, ensuring the retention of diversity and inclusion indicators becomes paramount. To truly advance our understanding without jeopardizing equitable representation and fair decision-making, we must constantly question our assumptions, seek out the voices of marginalized groups, and resist the temptation to treat all phenomena as if they are inherently uniform or homogeneous. Only then can we build meaningful knowledge that is reflective of the multifaceted world in which we exist, paving the way for inclusive and innovative solutions that benefit all.

## Industry-specific Examples: Retaining Critical Information in Various Fields

Retaining critical information during abstraction processes is vital in various industries. Despite their distinct natures, the fields of healthcare, finance, and manufacturing share the common challenge of identifying and preserving essential details for optimal decision-making and operations. By illustrating examples from these industries, we can understand how abstraction techniques are employed while striving to retain crucial details.

In healthcare, physicians often rely on abstraction to manage large amounts of patient data. Medical professionals use diagnostic codes, abstracting symptoms and diseases to streamline documentation and communication. However, retaining critical information is essential to ensure accurate diagnoses and treatment plans. Consider a doctor analyzing a patient's electronic health record (EHR). The EHR may contain years of data, including diagnostic test results, medication prescriptions, and lifestyle habits. The physician must balance abstraction with retaining essential information to identify patterns and correlations relevant to the patient's condition. For example, an allergy warning must not be lost during clinical note summarization. This retention of critical information safeguards against potential adverse drug reactions while still maintaining a digestible and concise medical history.

Similarly, in finance, abstraction is used to synthesize large quantities of data and identify trends in market performance, asset management, and risk assessment. Portfolio management relies on extracting key financial indicators (such as price-to-earnings ratio, return on equity, and risk-adjusted return) while omitting less relevant details. In this context, retaining essential information involves understanding which metrics are most pertinent to investment objectives and risk tolerance. For instance, an investment manager may need to prioritize environmental, social, and governance (ESG) factors when constructing a sustainable investment portfolio. If such factors are obscured by other metrics during abstraction, the resulting portfolio may not meet the investor's ethical standards.

In manufacturing, abstraction finds its utility in managing the complexity of supply chains and production processes. Engineers often break down production systems into smaller, abstract components to simplify analysis and problem - solving. However, critical information about the interdependencies and relationships among subsystems must be preserved. Take, for example, the production and assembly of a car engine. If key details about material requirements or supplier timelines are lost during the abstraction process, it could result in supply shortages, production delays, and cost overruns. By retaining essential information, manufacturers can optimize their operations and ensure timely delivery of high - quality products.

From these examples, it is clear that abstraction in various industries must be approached mindfully, placing emphasis on preserving critical information. Identifying the most relevant details and retaining them in the abstraction process is crucial to avoid adverse outcomes, such as misdiagnoses, poor investment performance, or disrupted supply chains.

As we venture further into the realm of abstraction, it is essential to adapt our strategies and techniques to the varying demands of each industry. By constantly refining and evolving our critical thinking skills, we can extract the essential insights from a sea of information while simultaneously honing our precision to maintain balance. As abstraction continues to be a key component of decision - making and problem - solving, we must ensure that this powerful cognitive tool is employed responsibly and ethically across all fields.

In an ever - changing world, our ability to adapt and refine our abstract thinking will ultimately define the success of our endeavors. With the proper retention of critical information at its core, the art of abstraction paves the path for a future where complex problems can be tackled with ease. The pursuit of balance in abstraction extends beyond mere mastery of a skill; it exemplifies the mindful and nuanced approach necessary for navigating the intricacies of our increasingly interdependent and interconnected global society.

## Applying Retention Techniques in Practical Frameworks: AI Product Roadmap and Data Flywheel

One key aspect of retaining essential details in AI product development is identifying what constitutes 'critical' information. For instance, in designing intelligent personal assistants or chatbots, it is vital to store essential patterns or rules about natural language semantics and syntax while eliminating redundant or irrelevant elements. As an AI product developer, you should have a comprehensive understanding of the domain-specific knowledge to make informed decisions about what information to preserve and what to discard.

To illustrate the application of retention techniques in AI product development, let's consider an example of developing an AI-based recommendation engine for an online e-commerce platform. In this scenario, the critical information includes user preferences, demographic information, past purchase history, and product details. As a developer, you need to be cautious not to lose these details during the abstraction process while generalizing user categories and product data. Additionally, maintaining the accuracy and consistency of the data pipeline is critical for an effective recommendation system. Identifying the essential features and ensuring their retention can significantly impact the quality of the AI product.

Incorporating retention techniques in Data Flywheel helps tackle data management challenges and accelerates the process of training AI models effectively. The concept of a Data Flywheel revolves around creating a self-sustaining virtuous cycle, whereby having better data attracts users, leading to more data being generated, ultimately resulting in improved AI models. Retaining critical information allows data-driven decisions that exhibit a greater degree of accuracy.

When working with diverse and voluminous datasets, striking a balance between discarding redundant information and preserving essential data attributes becomes critical. For instance, when dealing with user-generated data from various sources like social media, IoT devices, or mobile applications, certain information such as user preferences, sentiment analysis, and usage patterns could be categorized as crucial. Retaining these pieces of information while discarding unnecessary 'noise' in the data will allow the Data Flywheel to remain efficient and effective.

Additionally, ensuring diversity and inclusion in data is crucial during the data retention process. In the AI Product Roadmap, developers must carefully consider diverse user perspectives and avoid any potential bias in the data collection and analysis pipeline. This practice aids in building AI models that cater to a more comprehensive user base, making the AI product more inclusive and robust. Similarly, in the Data Flywheel, diverse datasets can provide a broader understanding and expose the AI models to varied data patterns, enhancing the overall data processing capability.

Applying retention techniques in AI Product Roadmap and Data Flywheel is indeed a challenging task that demands a clear distinction between critical information and unnecessary details. It requires developers and AI specialists to have the vision and expertise to identify and prioritize domain -specific knowledge and data attributes.

In conclusion, retaining critical information in abstraction is a fundamental aspect of designing and implementing successful AI products and data strategies. The ability to discern, capture, and optimize essential details lends a competitive edge to AI-driven solutions, ensuring they are well-equipped to deal with the complexities of real-world scenarios. Mastering the art of information retention while abstracting can undoubtedly propel AI product development and data management efforts to new heights, unlocking new potentialities in the ever-evolving field of artificial intelligence.

## Ensuring Responsible and Ethical Abstraction with Critical Information Retention

To frame the discussion, imagine a healthcare technology company developing an AI-powered medical diagnosis tool. The system relies on abstracting various medical data types, such as lab results, imaging studies, and patient demographics, to create predictive models for various diseases. To abstract the data efficiently, the development team must determine the essential details required to accurately diagnose patients without excluding information that could lead to inaccurate or biased predictions.

The first step in ensuring responsible and ethical abstraction involves identifying critical information and distinguishing it from superfluous material. One approach is to prioritize features with strong correlations to the desired outcomes, known as feature importance in machine learning.

Moreover, involving subject matter experts in the abstraction process can help identify the critical details that algorithmic methods might miss. While many details in a dataset may provide insights, retaining only essential information reduces the risk of overfitting and improves the model's generalizability.

Aside from retaining critical information, addressing potential biases in abstraction is essential in promoting fairness and inclusivity. In our medical diagnosis tool example, biases may emerge from unbalanced datasets during the data abstraction process. For instance, if the data overwhelmingly represents specific demographic groups or only considers symptoms that pertain to certain populations, the AI tool could potentially generate biased predictions. Engaging in practices such as targeted data collection or implementing fairness-aware algorithms can help mitigate such biases and ultimately lead to more ethical abstraction.

Another ethical concern arising from abstraction is its potential impact on human dignity and autonomy. For instance, overly simplistic abstraction could result in dehumanizing or stereotyping patients in medical settings, consequently affecting treatment options and clinical decision-making. To address this issue, responsible abstraction entails preserving crucial human traits within abstracted data, thereby upholding respect for individuals and the nuances of their experiences.

To ensure that abstraction remains cognizant of societal complexities, teams must cultivate a culture of introspection and continuous learning. By examining potential sources of bias and ethical concerns throughout the abstraction process, teams can iteratively refine their methods, ensure diversity and inclusivity indicators, and make abstraction more equitable. Additionally, encouraging open discussions among team members about ethical considerations can facilitate the surfacing of potential issues and foster a mindset of responsible abstraction.

Collaboration and knowledge-sharing across interdisciplinary teams will further support responsible abstraction practices. For example, specialists in fields such as ethics, behavioral science, or bias mitigation can lend invaluable insights to help identify and counterbalance any potential issues in the abstraction process. By incorporating diverse perspectives, teams can maintain more equitable, accountable, and transparent approaches to abstraction.

In closing, as abstraction continues to shape the development of innovative technologies and drive decision-making in countless fields, vigilance in ensuring responsible and ethical practices is paramount. By identifying and retaining essential information, addressing biases, fostering a culture of introspection and collaboration, and maintaining a strong ethical foundation, teams can harness the power of abstraction to create solutions that work for all. Responsible abstraction is not just an end goal, but a dynamic process that demands continuous reevaluation and mindful adaptation to a changing world. Through this commitment to ethical abstraction, society will advance technological frontiers without losing sight of its responsibility to ensure fairness, inclusivity, and respect for human dignity.

## Continuous Improvement: Adapting and Learning to Retain Essential Details in Abstraction Processes

The art of retaining essential details in abstraction lies at the heart of finding clever solutions to complex problems and making thoughtful decisions in today's rapidly evolving world. Just as a skilled sculptor must understand the balance between removing excess material and preserving the delicate features that give a work of art its identity, so too must we learn to adapt and evolve our approach to abstraction. By adopting an attitude of continuous improvement, we can hone our ability to separate the signal from the noise and develop a clear, nuanced understanding of the systems we hope to tame and control.

While adaptability is a virtue in virtually any domain, the drive for continuous improvement is especially crucial in a field as multifaceted and intricate as abstraction. The complex dance between simplification and retention of critical information presents an ongoing challenge, one that calls for a nimble mindset, a healthy dose of introspection, and a willingness to learn from both successes and missteps.

Take, for example, the case of designing an AI-powered urban traffic management system. One approach might be to break down the system into separate modules for signal timings, traffic monitoring, and incident response. In abstracting the overall problem, an engineer might strip away certain details, such as the specific configuration of each traffic light or the types of vehicles using the roads. A system that overzealously disregards critical information, however - such as the pedestrian patterns around schools or the locations of emergency service facilities - may ultimately fail to deliver the desired improvements in traffic flow and safety. In such a scenario, the key to achieving the best possible system lies in continuously refining the model, incorporating fresh insights, and adapting the abstraction process to retain the most critical information.

So, how can one pursue continuous improvement in abstraction, especially when focusing on the retention of essential details? Let us consider a few proven strategies that span various domains and cater to different learning styles.

One effective approach entails embracing the iterative nature of abstraction. Similar to the process of refining a hypothesis, tentative abstraction models should be subjected to rigorous examination, testing, and adjustment. In the software development world, techniques such as Agile methodologies and code review support this iterative mindset, resulting in cleaner, more maintainable code. Similarly, driven by curiosity and an acceptance of uncertainty, one can nurture an adaptive mindset in abstraction by maintaining an ongoing dialogue with colleagues, sharing ideas, and soliciting constructive feedback.

Another critical aspect of continuous improvement in abstraction is the cultivation of awareness and reflection. As we journey through various abstraction exercises, we will inevitably encounter situations where our initial abstraction breaks down, and essential details are inadvertently discarded. An adept practitioner will not only acknowledge these shortcomings but also take the opportunity to learn from them and refine their subsequent abstractions. Encounters with real - world systems that stubbornly resist abstraction - or reveal unforeseen complexities - can serve as valuable catalysts for growth, pushing us to adapt our models and explore fresh perspectives.

In addition to embracing iteration and reflection, a thoughtful abstractionist should also seek out diverse experiences and knowledge. Gaining exposure to multiple domains - whether through hands-on experimentation, academic study, or collaboration with domain experts - can provide fresh insights and teach valuable lessons in abstraction. By exploring how different fields approach the art of simplification, one can develop a versatile toolkit, borrow techniques from a wide array of disciplines, and cultivate a deeper understanding of the nuances of abstraction.

In pursuing continuous improvement, it is vital not to neglect the human element of abstraction. After all, behind every process of simplification lies an individual or team striving to make sense of the complexities of the world. By developing an empathetic, inclusive approach to abstraction, we can tune our work to the needs and contexts of diverse stakeholders and ensure that our models remain rooted in the realities they seek to represent. In doing so, we take the essential step of moving from an isolated, technical exercise in abstraction to creating a broader, richer understanding of the world.

As we adapt and learn to retain crucial details in our abstraction processes, let us remember that the art of simplification is not a static skill to be mastered, but rather a dynamic journey that constantly evolves to meet the challenges of our increasingly complex world. With courage, tenacity, and an openness to change, we can ride the currents of abstraction, craft elegant solutions to the most vexing problems, and open new frontiers of understanding.

# Chapter 9

# Advancing Abstraction Skills: Reflection, Adaptation, and Continuous Learning

The pursuit of abstraction mastery is a lifelong journey. It requires not only a deep understanding of the various types and techniques of abstraction but also an ongoing commitment to reflection, adaptation, and continuous learning. In other words, advancing your abstraction skills is not merely about developing a repertoire of methods to employ when faced with complex problems; it is about cultivating a mindset that fosters continual growth, improvement, and innovation. This mindset helps one navigate the delicate balance between simplification and preserving essential details, as well as making thoughtful and ethical abstractions.

Reflection is a cornerstone of any learning endeavor, and the development of abstraction skills is no exception. By engaging in regular self-assessment and introspection, one becomes more aware of one's own thought processes and can better identify areas for improvement. Post-mortem analysis, retrospectives, and self-critique are powerful tools that can help streamline the reflection process. For example, after completing a software architecture project, you can hold a retrospective with your team to identify how different abstraction techniques were employed, where assumptions were questioned, and the effectiveness of the abstractions used.

Furthermore, by reflecting on the abstraction techniques applied in these situations, you can discover patterns that enlighten future decisions. For instance, you might realize the importance of tailoring your abstractions to specific contexts or tackling the potential biases lurking in your conceptualizations. Over time, this reflective practice will enable you to hone your intuition, identify your cognitive blind spots, and become more deliberate in your abstraction efforts.

Adaptation and flexibility, on the other hand, are essential to accommodating different contexts and situations. When faced with new challenges or domains, an adaptable mindset can help you expand your existing toolkit of abstraction techniques. By actively seeking feedback from peers, you can learn from diverse perspectives and experiences, incorporating new insights into your approach. For example, a software engineer seeking to improve their abstraction skills might consider attending a workshop on applying abstraction in supply chain management. By exploring new domains, one gains a deeper understanding of the ways in which abstraction can manifest, as well as the nuances and subtleties that accompany these manifestations.

Moreover, embracing change and adaptation fosters a sense of curiosity and humility. This perspective positions you to be receptive to innovation and new ideas, which can, in turn, fuel your continuous learning journey. Encouraging an experimental attitude is particularly valuable when evolving from one abstraction technique to another, such as transitioning from modular abstraction in software engineering to temporal abstraction in product development.

Continuous learning is the engine that drives the advancement of abstraction skills. Engaging in professional development opportunities, attending trainings, and collaborating with others can help refine one's understanding of abstraction and sharpen one's skills. Setting specific goals, tracking your progress, and celebrating your achievements can provide motivation and momentum for your learning journey.

There is, however, an aspect of learning that remains beyond the procedural: the personal. Developing your abstraction skills is intrinsically linked to introspection, self-awareness, and growth. This convergence of intellectual and personal development is encapsulated by an ancient philosopher's counsel to "know thyself." To truly advance in our understanding and application of abstraction, we must not only expand our knowledge and expose ourselves to new challenges but also uncover the contours of our own cognitive landscapes, embracing thoughtful reflection and self-discovery.

In the process of advancing your abstraction skills, a profound paradox emerges. As you peer deeper into the complexities of abstraction, you unveil layers of nuance and subtlety hidden beneath seemingly simple surfaces. The art of abstraction thus echoes the elegance of a Zen paradox: simplicity begets complexity, and complexity begets simplicity. By delving into this enigmatic heart of abstraction, you will find not only a toolbox for simplification and problem-solving but also a gateway to self-awareness, growth, and continuous learning.

## Evaluating Your Abstraction Skills: Assessing Competence, Introspection, and Identifying Areas for Improvement

The first step in evaluating one's abstraction skills is to perform a self-assessment of one's competence. This begins with an honest appraisal of one's knowledge, experience, and understanding of the different types of abstraction and their applications in various fields. A solid foundation in the underlying principles of abstraction, along with practical experience in implementing these principles, is essential for becoming an adept abstract thinker.

One way to gauge one's competence in abstraction is to assess how effectively one can solve problems or make decisions with the use of abstraction techniques. This involves applying abstraction methods to a specific challenge or problem and examining the efficacy of the solutions or insights derived from this process. It also means being able to communicate the rationale behind the chosen level of abstraction and its implications on the outcomes. A strong understanding of the nuances of abstraction allows for its effective application when faced with complex, real-world issues.

Introspection is an integral part of the self-assessment process. This entails examining one's thought processes and patterns, as well as reflecting on past experiences involving abstraction. Introspection encourages a heightened self-awareness, enabling the identification of biases, blind spots, or gaps in understanding that may have affected one's abstraction abilities.

The process of introspection can be facilitated through various techniques, such as journaling, quiet reflection, or engaging in conversations with trusted colleagues or mentors. In doing so, one can unearth valuable insights and pinpoint specific aspects of one's abstraction skills that require further development or fine-tuning.

Another effective approach for evaluating abstraction skills is to actively seek feedback from others. Requesting input from peers, colleagues, or mentors regarding one's performance, particularly in the context of specific projects or challenges, can provide valuable insights into areas requiring improvement. Feedback should be appreciated as an opportunity for growth, as it uncovers blind spots that may hinder one's ability to abstract effectively.

Observing others who excel in abstraction can also prove instructive. Analyzing their processes, decision-making, and problem-solving abilities through the lens of abstraction can offer an arsenal of strategies, tips, and techniques that can be adopted and adapted to strengthen one's own skills.

Once areas for improvement have been identified, it is essential to develop a strategic plan to address them. This may involve pursuing additional education or training, participating in online or offline forums or workshops on abstraction, or simply dedicating time for focused practice on specific techniques. As with any skill, repetition is crucial in honing one's abilities, and consistent practice will lead to an organic growth in one's expertise in abstraction.

In conclusion, developing expertise in abstraction is a lifelong pursuit, requiring a blend of introspection, self-assessment, and persistence. The more inquisitive and reflective one is about one's skills, the more adept one becomes in utilizing abstraction as a powerful problem-solving tool. Like a skilled gardener tending to their garden, the abstract thinker must care for their cognitive abilities and skills, pruning away faulty techniques and nurturing the seeds of new ideas and approaches to blossom into fruitful solutions. The rewards of such diligent cultivation are well worth the effort, as a mastery of abstraction unlocks untold potential, generating novel insights and perspectives that lay the groundwork for innovation, discovery, and human progress.

## Reflection Techniques: Post - Mortem Analysis, Retrospectives, and Self - Critique in Abstraction Practice

The art of abstraction, as exemplified in various fields such as computer science, product development, and strategic planning, serves as a potent tool for managing complexity and simplifying intricate problems. However, one might uncover hidden weaknesses and areas for improvement within their abstraction practice by occasionally taking a step back and reflecting upon their experiences.

Three powerful but distinct reflection techniques can be employed to aid in this process of self-assessment and continuous improvement: post-mortem analysis, retrospectives, and self - critique. By leveraging these techniques in synergy, individuals can refine their abilities in abstract thinking, manage complexities better, and become more effective problem solvers.

Post - mortem analysis is a well - known practice conducted after the completion of a project, often involving a collaborative discussion among team members to discern the successes and failures that transpired. Within the context of abstraction, a post - mortem analysis can be conducted after the implementation of an abstraction - driven solution, delving deep into whether the appropriate level of abstraction was chosen, if the right tradeoffs were made, and if the assumptions made during the abstraction process effectively held up.

To illustrate this, let us consider the development of complex software systems, where teams often employ both modular and functional abstraction techniques. During the post - mortem analysis, questions could arise on the partitioning of system components, the organization of abstraction layers, the efficiency of the chosen abstractions, and the maintainability of the resulting system. This exercise can unearth valuable lessons that enrich the future application of abstraction techniques in similar initiatives.

The second reflection technique, retrospectives, borrows from agile methodologies, where teams periodically gather to review and assess their progress, streamline processes, and adapt to evolving contexts. Unlike post - mortem analyses, which occur only at a project's conclusion, retrospectives encourage ongoing reflection throughout the project lifecycle. By incorporating retrospectives in the context of abstraction, one can assess the ongoing impact of the abstraction techniques adopted, ensuring they remain relevant and effective as the project evolves.

A case in point is the utilization of physical abstraction in the development of an autonomous vehicle, involving abstraction layers to represent and manipulate sensor data and intricate control systems. Frequent retrospectives can help the development team evaluate the efficacy of these abstraction layers, making adjustments when necessary, ensuring the design aligns with both current data and anticipated future scenarios.

The final reflective technique, self-critique, involves a more personal, internal assessment of one's own abstraction skills and biases. By engaging in self-reflection, practitioners can scrutinize decisions made during abstraction and actively question the assumptions and simplifications made. Are essential details captured appropriately? Are there cognitive biases influencing the choices made during abstraction? Is there a hidden preference for certain abstractive techniques over others? These self-directed inquiries can reveal areas of improvement that may have otherwise gone unnoticed.

To exemplify self-critique, consider a product manager utilizing temporal and recursive abstractions to analyze a time-series dataset for forecasting trends that drive strategic decisions. By reflecting on their choices, such as the use of different temporal aggregation levels or the incorporation of recursive patterns, the product manager can identify bias, blind spots, or assumptions that may lead to suboptimal decisions.

Ultimately, artful abstraction is not about reaching a state of fixed mastery but rather about embracing the dynamic process of learning, growth, and self-improvement. Through post-mortem analyses, retrospectives, and self-critique, individuals and teams can reflect on their experiences, reevaluate their assumptions, and perpetually refine their abstraction practice. This reflective journey moves us one step closer to the sweet spot where complexity is managed with elegance, and deep and unsolved mysteries unpuzzle themselves with one simple stroke of genius.

## Adapting Your Abstraction Strategies: Incorporating Feedback, Refining Techniques, and Expanding Your Toolkit

One of the hallmarks of effective abstraction is an iterative mindset. Iteration involves an ongoing cycle of feedback, reflection, and refinement. One way to incorporate feedback into your abstraction strategy is through the use of communal resources, such as online forums, workshops, or collaboration within a professional network. These platforms offer a treasure trove of insights, critiques, and alternative perspectives to inform your method of abstract thinking.

When engaging in such environments, maintain an open mind, and be receptive to feedback that challenges your assumptions or existing techniques. Embrace the opportunity to evaluate the merits of others' perspectives, and weigh their potential utility for your unique problem-solving situations. By doing so, you not only expand your abstraction toolkit but also strengthen your adaptability in approaching complex problems from multiple angles.

Another approach to refining your techniques is through the critical analysis of relevant case studies, both successful and unsuccessful ones. By dissecting real-world examples, you gain invaluable insights into the nuances and intricacies of applying abstraction across various domains. Identifying patterns and commonalities, as well as pitfalls and limitations, arms you with the foresight to make more informed decisions when tackling similar problems.

For instance, consider the application of modular abstraction techniques in the development of a software system. Observing how efficient and scalable module design contributes to its overall performance can inform your own deployment of modular abstractions in future projects. On the other hand, understanding how a haphazardly abstracted system can result in inter-module dependencies and bottlenecks serves as a cautionary tale for avoiding such shortcomings in your own work.

Embracing experimentation is another valuable avenue for honing your abstraction skills. Grant yourself the freedom to test various levels of abstraction and gauge their efficacy in specific problem-solving scenarios. Consider conducting controlled experiments, by documenting your thought process and measuring the effectiveness of different abstraction techniques against a set of predefined criteria. This systematic approach allows you to identify strengths and weaknesses in your methodology and adapt accordingly.

Expanding your toolkit also entails forming connections with other fields and disciplines. As the adage goes, "the best way to have a new idea is to expose yourself to new ideas." Become a voracious learner, seeking out opportunities to engage with individuals from diverse domains and backgrounds.

Engage in vigorous discussions, attend conferences and industry events, and read books and articles from a wide range of subjects. Familiarizing yourself with the unique challenges and abstraction techniques employed in various fields equips you with a more diverse and versatile toolkit for approaching problem-solving situations.

Imagine, for example, a software engineer immersing themselves in the field of graphic design. By learning how visual artists employ abstraction to create aesthetically pleasing imagery, the software engineer acquires a new perspective on designing user interfaces and data visualizations. In turn, this enriched understanding of abstract thinking opens doors to innovative solutions and cross-domain collaboration.

As our journey through abstraction strategies comes full circle, we are reminded of the quotation by American author Eric Hoffer: "In a time of drastic change, it is the learners who inherit the future." By embracing feedback, refining our techniques, and expanding our toolkit, we commit ourselves to a lifelong journey of growth and improvement as abstract thinkers. Through this deliberate pursuit of progress, we stand ready to face the ever-evolving complexities of our world, equipped with the skills and insights needed to navigate the challenges that lie ahead. It is our collective hope that this odyssey of abstraction not only enriches our problem-solving capabilities but also fosters a deeper understanding of the intricate tapestry that is the human experience.

## Continuous Learning in Abstraction: Exploring New Domains, Attending Trainings, and Engaging in Professional Development

One of the most effective ways of enhancing your abstraction capabilities is through the exploration of new domains. Diversifying your knowledge and experiences will help you recognize patterns and shared structures across different fields, augmenting your ability to identify valuable insights. Mixing seemingly unrelated domains can facilitate the emergence of innovative perspectives, fostering an interdisciplinary approach to abstraction. For example, learning about functional programming in computer science can enrich an engineer's modularity skills when working on a hardware system. As you cultivate this intellectual agility, you will find immense value in drawing from a diverse array of disciplines, constantly refining your abstraction practice.

In addition, attending various training programs and workshops that focus on abstraction can significantly improve your expertise. These educational opportunities may target a specific technique, such as functional abstraction, or provide a broader treatment of the cognitive and metacognitive foundations of abstract thinking. By participating in these events, you will be exposed to new developments and best practices in the field, refining your skills, and expanding your toolbox of abstraction methods. Engaging in conversations with fellow practitioners during these events can be equally enlightening, providing valuable insights into how others utilize abstraction in their respective fields.

Professional development is another avenue through which you can heighten your abstraction abilities. Pursuing advanced degrees or certifications related to abstraction, from computer science to design strategy, can help you acquire a sophisticated understanding of the field. Your mastery over the intricacies of abstraction will be accentuated by collaborating on research projects, publishing articles, and speaking at conferences. Not only will this deepen your knowledge, but it will also help you establish a thought leadership presence in abstraction, inspiring others to follow suit.

As you continue to pursue professional development, consider networking with key influencers, academics, and practitioners within the abstraction space. Associating with likeminded individuals can spark interesting discussions, develop collaborative opportunities, and offer unique perspectives. Joining or forming communities of practice online or at the local level can further foster the exchange of knowledge and ideas, nurturing both collective wisdom and individual growth.

Committing to continuous learning in abstraction should not be limited to formal education and networking; an innate curiosity and a critical mind can incite learning in small yet profound ways. Observing the world around you and practicing discernment in drawing connections or contemplating the abstract will keep your cognitive muscles limber. Remain receptive to new ideas and practices from various sources, be it books, blogs, or podcasts, as they can offer fresh approaches and invaluable insights.

So, go forth, fellow abstractionist - let the horizon beckon, and the unknown be your muse. For it is in the pursuit of the seemingly elusive that you shall uncover peculiar parallels, spawn innovative syntheses, and ultimately, master the magnificent language of abstraction. And as your mastery blossoms over time, you will discover a universe of opportunities - a cosmos of connections, a landscape of lucid links - empowering you to wield abstraction not just as a technique, but also as an art form that can transform the way you perceive and navigate the world.

## Measuring Progress and Success: Tracking Improvement, Setting Goals, and Celebrating Achievements in Abstraction Mastery

To begin with, we must first establish a clear understanding of the key skills involved in abstraction mastery. Some essential skills include:

1. Identifying and extracting essential details from complex scenarios 2. Breaking down problems into manageable units (modular abstraction) 3. Employing context - dependent thinking to adapt abstraction techniques to the situation at hand 4. Challenging assumptions and avoiding false dichotomies 5. Retaining critical information while simplifying problems 6. Applying various abstraction forms across disciplines effectively

A well - structured evaluation process involves a mix of quantitative and qualitative methods. Let's explore some techniques that can help assess each of these skills.

For assessing the first three skills, it can be beneficial to periodically engage in problem - solving exercises or projects. To measure the progress in these domains, one may analyze the efficiency of their solutions, solicit feedback from peers and mentors, and keep a log of lessons learned. Comparing previous solutions with more recent ones can reveal growth, as well as areas that require further work.

For developing context - dependent thinking, an essential practice can involve intentionally placing oneself in unfamiliar situations or exploring new fields. Journaling your thoughts and experiences can provide insights into how well you've managed to adapt and extract essential information in an unfamiliar domain. Additionally, reflection on past successes and failures can prove insightful in evaluating one's progress in questioning assumptions and breaking false dichotomies.

Retaining critical information in abstraction is inherently challenging due to the process's nature of simplifying problems. A self-assessment exercise can involve revisiting past projects from different fields and identifying instances where critical information was missed or discarded. Comparing improvements in recent projects relative to older ones can provide a measure of progress in this area.

Another valuable technique to measure improvement across various abstraction forms is to adopt a goal-setting approach. The SMART criteria (Specific, Measurable, Attainable, Relevant, and Time-bound) can be applied when constructing goals for your abstraction skillset. For instance, a concrete goal may be "improve my physical abstraction skills by modeling the behavior of a novel system within three months." Progress can be tracked by breaking the goal into smaller milestones and reflecting on the results of your efforts.

Celebrate your achievements in abstraction mastery by acknowledging milestones reached, big or small. For example, upon successfully abstracting a complex problem that once seemed insurmountable or utilizing a new technique in a different discipline effectively. Recognizing and celebrating these moments not only fuels motivation and personal growth but also solidifies the knowledge and skills acquired.

In conclusion, measuring progress and success in abstraction mastery is an ongoing and multifaceted journey. By assessing one's performance across various aspects of abstraction and investing in the right evaluation techniques, you can better understand your strengths and weaknesses, ultimately achieving mastery. As a mindful abstraction practitioner, embrace continuous improvement, growth, and celebrate your accomplishments along the way. Your journey towards abstraction mastery is not only beneficial for your problem-solving prowess but also contributes to the advances made in your chosen field, pushing boundaries and unveiling new horizons for yourself and others.